Tyndale online at www.tyndale.com.

Tyndale Momentum online at www.tyndalemomentum.com.

DALE and *LeatherLike* are registered trademarks of Tyndale
se Publishers, Inc. *Tyndale Momentum*, the Tyndale Momentum
and *365 Pocket* are trademarks of Tyndale House Publishers,

Walk Thru the Bible logo is a registered trademark of Walk Thru
Bible Ministries, Inc.

Pocket Devotions: Inspiration and Renewal for Each New Day

ted from *At His Feet* (2003) under ISBN 978-0-8423-8125-3
The One Year Walk with God Devotional (2004) under
978-1-4143-0056-6 by Tyndale House Publishers, Inc.

gned by Beth Sparkman

ed by Karin Buursma

N 978-1-4143-8789-5

ted in China

18 17 16 15 14 13
6   5   4   3   2   1

365 Pocket™ Devotions

Inspiration and Renewal for Each New Day

CHRIS TIEGREEN

An I...
Tyndale Hous...

INTRODUCTION

When you spend time with God, something incredible happens. As you take a few moments to pause from the stress and hurry of everyday life to focus on God and His plan for you, you become more centered, refreshed, and at peace. Meeting with God every day transforms you. And as you grow closer to Him, you'll have access to His guidance and wisdom for all the daily decisions you face.

That's what the inspirational readings in this book are all about: renewing your soul so you can better understand yourself, your world, and your God.

In this book you will find 365 devotions first created for Walk Thru the Bible, an international ministry dedicated to igniting passion for God's Word. The selections are arranged by days and topics. You can read through each day of the year consecutively if you wish. Alternatively, look in the index for a topic that will provide wisdom and guidance about something you may be experiencing that very day. Every few days you will also find shorter readings. These are devotions for days when time is limited.

Thank you for joining us on this quest for a deeper devotional life. It is our hope that by the end of this book, you will feel as if you have gained greater understanding about God and His Word and—most important—feel closer to Him than ever before.

☼ A reflection on KNOWING GOD
When I want to have a closer relationship with God

When we come to Jesus, we often come with only our perceived needs on our minds—our circumstances, our health, our direction. We receive no rebuke from Him when we do. His words are gentle and comforting. But He also takes the opportunity to teach us about Himself. In fact, He may allow deep needs to surface in our lives specifically so we will come to Him for help and learn about Him in the process.

God's first purpose for us is spiritual wholeness—healing from the crippling disease of sin. Faith in Jesus is the key to receiving healing from God, and the Son of Man has authority over everything that afflicts us.

We come to the wonder-worker for a miracle. We leave knowing God. He is not content just helping us get by in this world and meeting only the needs we think we have. He who offers us Himself will not rest until we get up and go home knowing Him and His authority.

Some people brought to him a paralyzed man on a mat. Seeing their faith, Jesus said to the paralyzed man, "Be encouraged, my child! Your sins are forgiven."
MATTHEW 9:2

❂ A reflection on REGRET
When I feel paralyzed because of my past

Regrets can haunt us and keep us preoccupied with the past. Yet two truths will keep the past from stealing our joy in the present: our identification with Jesus and our faith in God's sovereignty. We must remember that we stand before God on the basis of what *He* has done, not what we have done. And we can trust that God knew about our mistakes before the foundation of the world and planned to compensate accordingly. Nothing we've done has surprised Him. God never asked us to look back and lament about our shortcomings. We confessed when we came to Jesus that we were sinful failures, and He saved us. It's time to move forward.

Do memories of the past hound you? Take an active stance against them. Be assured that the enemy's accusations are irrelevant once you've found your identity in the perfect Son of God. Find heroes of the faith in Scripture who failed—it's a pretty easy task—and see how God sovereignly worked out His purposes in spite of their failures. Rest in the present and look forward with hope. Nothing in your past can thwart God's plan.

Forgetting the past and looking forward to what lies ahead,
I press on to reach the end of the race.
PHILIPPIANS 3:13-14

DAY 3

☀ **A reflection on LIGHT**
 When I need Jesus to illuminate my thinking

Jesus is the only light this world has ever seen. We can't find illumination anywhere else. He's the One through whom God once said, "Let there be light," and there was light. We're the ones who shrouded this planet in a sinful haze of spiritual blindness. He came back into it with all the radiance of a million suns.

Plato told an allegory of people in a cave who saw each other as shadows. They thought they could see clearly enough, because shadows were all they knew. Like Plato's cave dwellers, we think we're well informed; and when we encounter light, we feel the pain of brightness in our maladapted eyes. We turn back to the darkness we're so comfortable with.

This world no longer has anything to offer you. Its interpretations of life are but shadows; its knowledge is untouched by the light of truth. Reject it. Do you really want understanding? Open your mind exclusively to Jesus and let Him shine.

[Jesus said,] "I have come as a light to shine in this dark world, so that all who put their trust in me will no longer remain in the dark." JOHN 12:46

☀ A reflection on GOD'S PLAN
When I wonder about His goal for the world

Have you ever wondered what God's plan is? There is no clearer statement of His primary goal than Matthew 24:14, which tells us that history is about the Kingdom of God and its proclamation among all peoples. And when the Kingdom has drawn its members from every people group, Jesus will announce the end of human history.

As believers, we do not drift through history. We are given a goal. We are to point to Christ, the sum of all things (Colossians 1:16-18).

Where is your life pointed? Is it consistent with the goal of history that God has made plain? The beauty of His story is that we can be involved in history's progress toward its climax. We are allowed to be colaborers with God in His plan for this world. Everything we do must be for the building up of His Kingdom. Everyone must be involved in its proclamation to all peoples. Every eye must watch for His coming again. We can choose the right direction because we know something the world doesn't know—how the story ends.

The Good News about the Kingdom will be preached throughout the whole world, so that all nations will hear it; and then the end will come.
MATTHEW 24:14

DAY 5

☼ A reflection on GRATITUDE
When I want my thankfulness to God to overflow

Nine lepers accepted the generous gift of Jesus and walked away without saying "Thank you." But the tenth—a Samaritan—gave thanks. He likely had been brought up to believe that Samaritans were outcasts, rejected by God's people and alien to His Kingdom. He would have understood his cleansing to be an amazing gift of grace. He expressed his gratitude by throwing himself at Jesus' feet and praising God with a loud voice.

How have we responded to our healing? When God cleansed us of sin, did we accept it politely, as though we were entitled to it? Many of us who were raised in the church think of salvation this way. We see it as an obligatory gift. We take it for granted.

Those who have truly known their diseased condition are often shameless and persistent—even embarrassing—in their gratitude. And this is exactly the attitude Jesus commends. He welcomes exuberance. More than anything, it reflects a genuine understanding of His grace.

One of them, when he saw that he was healed, came back to Jesus, shouting, "Praise God!" He fell to the ground at Jesus' feet, thanking him for what he had done. This man was a Samaritan. LUKE 17:15-16

DAY 6

☸ A reflection on IDOLATRY
When I am trying to serve both God and something else

Does Jesus contend with any rivals in our lives? Do we have any "gods" before Him? We may not know the answer to this until He asks us to give one up. Consider this sentence: "You cannot serve both God and _____."
Let someone fill in the blank with every rival he or she can think of and then measure the defensiveness of your reaction. This may show where God wants to work in your life.

No one can serve two masters. MATTHEW 6:24

DAY 7

☸ A reflection on GREATNESS
When I need to become like a child

Have you learned that status in the Kingdom of God is an inverted version of status in the world? The first will be last and the last first (Matthew 20:16). Those who wish to rule must serve (Matthew 20:26). And the greatest in the Kingdom of Heaven has aspired to the humility of . . . well, just a child. Aspire to greatness—the greatness of being discounted like a child. It's the way up in the Kingdom.

Anyone who becomes as humble as this little child is the greatest in the Kingdom of Heaven. MATTHEW 18:4

DAY 8

☀ **A reflection on ACCOUNTABILITY**
When I need to consider carefully how I am using my life

We are accountable to our Creator. He sees us, and one day we will stand before Him to explain what we have done and what we have left undone. We will have to own up to every thoughtless comment (Matthew 12:36), and we will have to explain the discrepancy between the resources we've been given and the resources we've used.

This can be a frightening thought, but it is not meant to frighten us. Before our accounting, we who believe have already been given assurance of forgiveness in Christ. Yet one day at the end of our earthly lives, we will stand before God with a full understanding that we had the power of Jesus Himself working within us, and an acute awareness that we did so little with it.

These words are not for judgment, they are for encouragement. God gives them to stir us up. They prompt us to live with an understanding of whose we are and why we were made. Let the truth of God's ownership sink in. When it does, it changes everything. Your life will never be the same.

The LORD sees clearly what a man does, examining every path he takes. PROVERBS 5:21

DAY 9

☀ A reflection on LOVING OTHERS
When I need to follow Christ's example

Jesus told His disciples that He was giving them a new commandment: to love one another. Have you ever asked yourself what is new about this commandment? What element of it was not already given in the Old Testament? The commandment to love our neighbors as ourselves was prominent in Jewish theology before Jesus came. It's scriptural from all the way back in Leviticus (19:18). So what's new?

Jesus clarifies after His initial statement: We are to love one another as He has loved us. That's what is different. That's more than loving our neighbors as ourselves. That's making deep, painful sacrifices for them. It is a matter of seeking their good above our own. No prior commandment has made such specific claims on us, defining for us what real love is. No definition will suffice in teaching us what kind of love this is; only an illustration will do. And the illustration is Jesus. The way He loved us is the way we are to love others.

I am giving you a new commandment: Love each other. Just as I have loved you, you should love each other.
JOHN 13:34

☀ A reflection on LIVING IN THE SPIRIT
When I am frustrated with my own efforts

We cannot become mature disciples except by supernatural means. Jesus did not come into this world to make us better; He came into this world to make us new. There's a significant difference.

We know what a mature Christian looks like. He or she will have the fruit of the Spirit: love, joy, peace, patience, kindness, goodness, faithfulness, gentleness, and self-control (Galatians 5:22-23). What we don't seem to know—or we forget easily—is that we don't grow these attributes by doing our best at them. We get them by realizing how foreign they are to our human nature, how futile our attempts at achieving them are, and how dependent on God we are for His life within us.

Are you frustrated with your Christian growth? No amount of human effort can fulfill God's laws. You were born of the Spirit when you believed. Now live by the Spirit. Cry out to God for Him to live His life in you, and He will accomplish your righteousness.

After starting your Christian lives in the Spirit, why are you now trying to become perfect by your own human effort?
GALATIANS 3:3

☼ A reflection on WORKS
When I am tempted to think that my status depends on what I do

God is gracious and He blesses us with innumerable and invaluable blessings. Jesus is clear about that. But He is also clear that we can never come to God with a sense of entitlement to those blessings. We can never say, "God, I've behaved well. Why are You treating me this way?" To do so indicates that at some level, we still think our standing with God is dependent on our performance. It isn't. Our standing with God is dependent on Christ's performance, and we are forever indebted.

God is intensely interested in our works. Our performance does matter to Him, but only as a response of faith, not as an act of merit. Our attitude of service indicates the degree to which the gospel has penetrated our hearts. And if it has truly penetrated our hearts, it will be humble service indeed.

Does the master thank the servant for doing what he was told to do? Of course not. In the same way, when you obey me you should say, "We are unworthy servants who have simply done our duty." LUKE 17:9-10

DAY 12

☼ **A reflection on WISDOM**
   When I consider the value of spiritual insight

Godly wisdom protects us from the self-inflicted disaster of superficial decisions. It keeps us from sacrificing ourselves to the deity of self-will. Throughout our lives, we must make repeated choices that will profoundly affect our own lives and the lives of those around us. The sooner we learn godly wisdom, the safer we will be. Wisdom protects us from futility.

We are given a very brief amount of time on this planet, but what we do here can have an eternal impact on ourselves and others. We must invest our time. We must invest our resources. We must direct everything at our disposal toward an eternal Kingdom. Without God's wisdom, years are wasted. We make self-defeating decisions. We squander opportunities to serve God and bear eternal fruit. Why should we never forsake wisdom? It's a matter of self-defense. It protects us from a world of evil, and it protects us from ourselves.

Don't turn your back on wisdom, for she will protect you.
PROVERBS 4:6

DAY 13

☼ A reflection on GOD'S WILL
When I am reluctant to give up my own agenda

When you pray for God's will to be done, you are actually praying for your own best interests to be accomplished. God's will for us never contradicts our own desire for blessing. His eternal perspective eminently qualifies Him to take us through difficult places when He knows the ultimate outcome will fulfill our heart's desires. Our vision is too limited to see this, so we hesitate to pray as Jesus instructed. But we will never be disappointed when we do.

May your will be done on earth, as it is in heaven.
MATTHEW 6:10

DAY 14

☼ A reflection on HUMILITY
When I need to be humble before God

Many Christians try to make a good impression on the world, thinking that God displays Himself in our righteousness. But God displays Himself better in our humility, where we are seen as needy and He is seen as merciful. The incredible truth of the gospel is that the way to be exalted is to fall facedown in repentance, crying out to God. It leaves nothing up to us and *everything* up to Him. There is no better place to be.

Those who humble themselves will be exalted.
LUKE 18:14

☼ A reflection on MERCY
When I need to appreciate God's abundant love for me

The greatest commandment of all, said Jesus, is to love God with everything we are and everything we have. It's what we were created for. But here, in the context of fallen humanity, our love is contingent on the mercy we have experienced. And where love is faint, mercy has been missed.

Does your love for God overflow with gratitude? Does it weep at His feet? If not, go back to the Cross. Contemplate the huge chasm that once lay between the deadness of your spirit and the life of your God. Remember the cold rebellion—that chilling apathy toward our Creator—that we all started out with. Understand that we were separated from any deserving claim on His goodness. Everything that brought us back to Him was all grace—nothing else. Pure, unbridled mercy. A love that knows no restraint and accepts no resistance.

Few people really understand God's mercy. Become one who does. Know the magnitude of His grace. And let your love for Him reflect it.

Her sins—and they are many—have been forgiven, so she has shown me much love. But a person who is forgiven little shows only little love. LUKE 7:47

DAY 16

☼ A reflection on PRIORITIES
When I am focused on material needs

We are told not to worry about what we will eat or drink. Yet we have that tendency because we get our priorities mixed up. We spend all our time trying to sustain ourselves so that we might experience and enjoy life. But we never get around to experiencing and enjoying life because we're spending all our time sustaining it. Our priorities are wrong.

God wants us to invest in what is valuable. Food and clothes are temporary. They are not valuable; they only support what is valuable—life. We act as though the wrapping is more important than the gift. We don't recognize real value.

What are we to do with mixed-up priorities and misplaced values? Lay them aside. Look at what God does with His birds and His lilies. They spend all their lives just "being" for the glory of God. We spend all our lives just "doing," usually for the glory of ourselves. We need Jesus to come along and radically revise our conception of things. He takes our upside-down thinking here and turns it upright, the way God intended it. Let us measure our priorities with those God has for us.

Isn't life more than food, and your body more than clothing?
MATTHEW 6:25

☀ A reflection on ENEMIES
When I am resentful toward others

So often we feel compelled to respond to others as they have dealt with us. When we have been mistreated, we cultivate bitterness and resentment about the experience. Jesus *never* says that these are not genuine or legitimate feelings. What He calls for, instead, is absolutely counter-intuitive to the human experience: a rejection of our resentments and bitterness, no matter how appropriate they are. We are to love even when love grates against our souls. While we hope for the downfall of our enemies, Jesus actually expects us to pray for blessings to rain down upon them. Why?

The Bible says we were once enemies of God (Romans 5:10; Colossians 1:21). And His response was to rain blessings upon us—the gift of salvation. Did this give us victory over God? Quite the contrary. God's blessing, in spite of our enmity with Him, made us humble. Neither will our blessing of our enemies give them the victory we think it will. Rather, it will demonstrate the grace of God. And we will be one step closer to being like Him.

I say, love your enemies! Do good to those who hate you. Bless those who curse you. Pray for those who hurt you.
LUKE 6:27-28

☼ A reflection on GOD'S WORD
When I need to be anchored in Scripture

In a world of shifting loyalties, devious cons, and ever-evolving ideas, we need to know where to anchor our souls. Only God can point us in the right direction. We need to be anchored in revelation. How do we do that?

A daily time in God's Word is a good first step. It works truth into our minds on a regular basis. But is that really enough to protect us against error?

Here's a good pattern to follow: First, ask God every day to convince your heart of His truth and to give you discernment. Second, find at least one verse a week to memorize. Chew on it, let it sink in, look at it from every angle, and come up with specific ways to apply it. Third, don't just study God's Word. Fall in love with it. God has a way of working into our hearts the things that we love. According to Colossians 3:16, we are to let the Word of Christ richly dwell within us. Let it richly dwell in you this week.

Every word of God proves true. He is a shield to all who come to him for protection. PROVERBS 30:5

☀ A reflection on UNITY
*When I need to seek genuine harmony among
other believers*

Most evangelistic training manuals and classes do not
include a session on the unity of the church. But right
before His passion, Jesus prays for His believers to be
one—completely united—*"that the world will know that
you sent me."* Such unity stands out because true, loving
fellowship is alien to this world.

Have you ever been in a fellowship in which "all the
believers were united in heart and mind" (Acts 4:32)? If
you have, you know that such a fellowship acts as a mag-
net to everyone around it. It grows deeper and often larger.
People are drawn to something they know to be supernatural; they marvel at unity because it does not come
from human impulse.

The genuine unity of the saints is the greatest tool of
evangelism God has given us. Do not seek others for the
Kingdom without seeking this as well.

*[Jesus said,] "May they experience such perfect unity that the
world will know that you sent me and that you love them as
much as you love me."* JOHN 17:23

DAY 20

✹ **A reflection on PRIORITIES**
When I want to invest my life in God's Kingdom

Where do you invest your life? In trying to maintain security and comfort in the next few decades, or in knowing the incorruptible glory of eternity? Millions will one day see all of their life's labor come to nothing. By contrast, what a blessing for those who are rich toward God! Consider the long term and examine where your investments lie. Use your resources for the coming Kingdom.

Life is not measured by how much you own. . . . A person is a fool to store up earthly wealth but not have a rich relationship with God. LUKE 12:15, 21

DAY 21

✹ **A reflection on TESTIFYING ABOUT GOD**
When I wonder how I can be an effective witness

We often think we need years of preparation and experience before we are useful to God. We don't. We often think God needs His witnesses to have sterling reputations. He doesn't. All that's required is this: an encounter with Jesus and willingness to tell about it. How we complicate things! Like the ex-demoniac Jesus healed, all we're asked to do is to "tell them everything the Lord has done" for us. It's that simple.

Go home to your family, and tell them everything the Lord has done for you and how merciful he has been.
MARK 5:19

☸ A reflection on DISCIPLESHIP
When I am counting the cost of following Jesus

The cost of discipleship is great. Jesus makes that point over and over again. He calls for a willingness to deny oneself and take up a cross. He called His disciples to suffer the cost.

But the cost of *not* following Jesus is even greater than the cost of discipleship. Those who do not follow Him—even those who follow Him, *but not wholeheartedly*—miss all of the blessings and benefits of being completely sold out to Christ. They miss intimate fellowship with the Creator of all that is; they miss the power of God at work in their lives; they miss the peace and fullness of knowing they are right with God. And they will miss great eternal rewards.

Every human being pays an extremely high price—either the cost of discipleship or the cost of opting out of it. The cost of opting out is infinitely greater. Holding on to a little bit of self destroys intimacy with God and renders a life relatively fruitless. Let go of your agenda and receive the blessing of walking in His steps in the power of His Spirit.

What do you benefit if you gain the whole world but lose your own soul? MATTHEW 16:26

DAY 23

☼ A reflection on BLESSING OTHERS
When I want to share God's goodness with others

There is a spiritual principle at work when we do anything in the Spirit, character, and name of Jesus. We were not created to be untapped reservoirs of His grace. We cannot store it up, and we cannot legitimately withhold it from others. But when we serve in humility, willingly taking a role that's inferior to the ones to whom we minister, we become like Jesus. In effect, we become channels of His blessing. His mercy flows out, and we are emptied enough to receive more of His mercy.

This is how Jesus does His work in this world. The church is His body; its members must do the things that He would do if He were here in the flesh. If His Spirit is in us, we will be like Him and we will act like Him. His Spirit will flow from us to a needy world, and His Spirit will flow into us because we have not been stingy with His grace. We receive blessing because we have blessed others.

I have given you an example to follow. Do as I have done to you. . . . Now that you know these things, God will bless you for doing them. JOHN 13:15, 17

☀ **A reflection on FORGIVENESS**
   When I am harboring a grudge

Nursing resentments and harboring grudges is such a pitiful human tendency, and yet we have all done it. We let offenses—large and small, real and imagined—rob us of the joy God means for us to have. How can we possibly understand God's forgiveness this way? When we focus on judgment and justice toward others, can we ever understand God's mercy toward us? Do we really imagine that those who have sinned against us have sinned greatly, while our offenses against God are minor and easy for Him to overlook? If so, we have it backward. Our sins against God, no matter how small, are offenses against the eternal, infinite Being. They therefore required an eternal, infinite sacrifice. Offenses against us pale in comparison.

Far from being a legal prerequisite for our own forgiveness, Jesus' command to forgive others prepares us to understand the gospel. The God of extravagant mercy asks us only to get a glimpse of His grace. Do you hold any grudges against others? Get a glimpse of God's mercy by forgiving them.

Do not condemn others, or it will all come back against you. Forgive others, and you will be forgiven. LUKE 6:37

☼ A reflection on WORDS
When I am aware of the power of the tongue

Words burn. Once they've ignited, there is no undoing them. Once spoken, words cannot be unspoken—and because of the gossip-prone nature of the human community, words spread rapidly. It is virtually impossible to put them out.

The tongue must be tamed! Its corruption both spreads outward and works inward. Words not only distort the perceptions of others, they train our own minds to follow. A careless comment becomes a deeply held conviction all too quickly. There is no such thing as idle chatter. Words matter.

How careful are you with your tongue? Biblical wisdom has much to teach us about the power of speech. "The things that come out of the mouth come from the heart, and these make a man 'unclean,'" Jesus said (Matthew 15:18, NIV). Words reveal our inner impurities, and those impurities may offend others. The childhood saying about sticks and stones simply isn't true. Words can hurt.

So guard your tongue. It can set the whole course of your life on fire, according to James. Anything with that kind of power must be tamed.

The tongue is a flame of fire. It is a whole world of wickedness, corrupting your entire body. It can set your whole life on fire. JAMES 3:6

☀ **A reflection on GUARDING MY HEART**
   *When I need to treasure what God has placed
   in my heart*

We typically think of guarding our heart in terms of keeping things out. Corruption, false ideas, temptations—all are to be held at arm's length. But there's another side to this vigilance. We are to keep things *in*—things like the spirit of Jesus, the humility and gentleness, the servanthood and sacrifice, the worship and thankfulness.

While most religions tell us to avoid the bad, God tells us to embrace Him. So guard the way out. Stand at the inside of the gate, and be careful about what may be leaving. Once in a while, we get a life-altering glimpse of true worship. By all means, keep it in! From time to time, we'll see a picture of true servanthood. Don't let that picture go! Occasionally, we are touched by a spirit of sacrifice, moved by a ministry, or convinced by a powerful word from the Lord. Hold on to these things! Treasuring the wellspring that God has birthed in your heart will leave little room for those corruptions you once obsessed over. And the wellspring is a much more pleasant preoccupation.

Guard your heart above all else, for it determines the course of your life. PROVERBS 4:23

DAY 27

☼ A reflection on UNANSWERED PRAYER
When God is not changing things the way I'd like

When God doesn't resolve a situation to our liking, especially a situation in which the suffering is great, we are tempted to accuse Him of either impotence or negligence. But we need to look within. Unanswered prayer is a call to come closer, know God better, and seek His will further. It is a call to be conformed to the image of Christ. By such the Father separates those who desire to test Him from those who desire to know Him.

Anything is possible if a person believes. MARK 9:23

DAY 28

☼ A reflection on LORDSHIP
When I need to recognize Christ's authority in my life

It is folly to call Jesus "Teacher," "Lord," or any other title that presumes His authority, and then to be casual about His authority in our lives. But such folly is so consistent with human nature. We convince ourselves that we believe something, even while our actions demonstrate otherwise. Examine the relationship between your faith and your way of life. Are they in sync? Are Jesus' radical words your driving force? Let Him truly be your Lord.

[Jesus said,] "You call me 'Teacher' and 'Lord,' and you are right, because that's what I am." JOHN 13:13

☼ A reflection on JESUS
When I need to affirm who He really is

We must ask ourselves the very question Jesus asked His disciples: Who do we really—deep in our hearts—believe Jesus is? This answer must be more than theology in our heads; it must be the truth that grips our hearts.

When your situation is dire—a relationship has broken, finances are looking impossibly bleak, a disease is pronounced incurable, or tragedy strikes a loved one—who is Jesus? Is He a theological tenet or really *your* Savior, *your* Provider, *your* Healer and Friend? When you are tempted beyond your strength—immoral desires are running rampant, an ethical compromise would seem so easy, or you are pressured to conform to the world's expectations—who is He? An ancient biblical character or *your* Righteousness, *your* Strength, and *your* Refuge?

Know Him in your innermost being. Jesus doesn't help us much as the center of our theology; He helps us as the center of our lives.

[Jesus] asked them, "Who do people say I am?" "Well," they replied, "some say John the Baptist, some say Elijah, and others say you are one of the other prophets." Then he asked them, "But who do you say I am?" MARK 8:27-29

DAY 30

☼ **A reflection on PEACE**
  When I need to set my hope on God

Worry is a plague. We know there is a place of peace and rest for the believer—Jesus has promised it to us. But how do we get there?

Jesus tells us to set our minds on the Kingdom. This is hard to do. In a crisis, we are prone to set our minds on the desired outcome. We fix our gaze on the preferred result and ask God to accomplish it. That outcome may be good and holy, but as long as it is our hope, we are not focused on Jesus and His Kingdom. Jesus asks us to set our minds on God and accept what He accomplishes. The outcome may be exactly the same in both cases, but calm in our hearts will only be a reality in the latter approach. We cannot experience the peace of faith when our eyes see God as a tool to accomplish our purposes. Our eyes can be either on God or on outcomes. Not both.

Pry your hopes off of your circumstances and put them on the Person who promises peace. Desire only Him, and you will never be disappointed—or worried.

Can all your worries add a single moment to your life?
LUKE 12:25

DAY 31

☼ A reflection on DELIGHTING IN GOD
When I am amazed that God can take pleasure in me

We live in an age in which many people think God is distant. We are amazed, then, when we learn that the relationship we are called to have with Him exceeds any other relationship in its level of intimacy. Not only is it true that God loves us and we are to love Him; He *delights* in us and we are to *delight* in Him. This in its fullness is the most pleasurable relationship we could possibly have—with anyone.

Meditate today on two Old Testament verses: "Take delight in the LORD" (Psalm 37:4) and "He will take delight in you with gladness. With his love, he will calm all your fears. He will rejoice over you with joyful songs" (Zephaniah 3:17). Think of that. God sings! Not just about anything, but about us! And He asks us to return the feeling. It's an amazing invitation.

This is the truth that shapes our hearts for a lifetime. An eternal lifetime. Allow it to do its work in you, and see your relationship with God transformed.

Take delight in the LORD, and he will give you your heart's desires. PSALM 37:4

☼ A reflection on THE HEAVENLY FATHER
When I am searching for significance

Jesus told His disciples that they would not be abandoned as orphans—and through them, He tells us the same. We have a Father. We may think that children of presidents, kings, and the rich and famous are in a privileged position. But their privilege doesn't match ours, because their parents do not match ours. *Our* Father is the author of all that is—even of their parents' fame and power. Jesus tells us to pray to the Almighty God as "Father," John tells us that God gave to those who believe in Jesus the right to become His children (John 1:12), and Paul says the Spirit of God's Son is in our hearts crying out, "Abba, Father" (Galatians 4:6).

Isn't it ridiculous that we search for significance in anything else? That's like trying to find beauty in graffiti when we've been offered the works of Michelangelo. Why would we persist in such an absurdity?

Are you feeling unimportant? Lonely? Discouraged? Empty? Directionless? You are *not* an orphan. Meditate on your role as a child of the Most High. Let it really sink in. Let it consume you. It's incredibly significant.

I will not abandon you as orphans—I will come to you.
JOHN 14:18

☀ A reflection on BELIEF

When I need courage to have faith in what I cannot see

We are constantly asked to stake our lives on an invisible God and a risen Savior whom we do not see. His footprints are all over history, so it isn't a baseless faith. But it is still often hidden to our five senses, and when we let those senses rule, we find the life of faith difficult.

How much of your walk with God is based on your five senses? Do you invest your heart in Him only when He is demonstrating His favor? Or do you trust that His love is real even when you don't see it? When the Bible says that God is a refuge, a help in trouble, a deliverer, a healer—and all the other wonderful things it says about Him—that revelation is a greater reality than the book you hold in your hand or anything else your eyes can see and fingers can touch. There is a profound blessedness in believing that. God manifests His Presence to those who believed Him before having seen Him. He readily intervenes on behalf of those who know He will. Believe, and be blessed.

Blessed are those who believe without seeing me.
JOHN 20:29

DAY 34

☼ A reflection on LOVE
When I want to model Christ's example

Is your love the kind that Jesus has? We cannot be convinced that His love truly dwells within us until we see ourselves behaving like Him. Do we love the unlovable? Do we sacrifice ourselves for others' good? Are we willing to pay any price—even to the point of death—that others might know His love? That is how His love behaves. It sacrifices.

You must have the same attitude that Christ Jesus had.
PHILIPPIANS 2:5

DAY 35

☼ A reflection on FAILURE
When I am discouraged by my weaknesses

We are apt to think that failure disqualifies us from serving God well. To the contrary, sometimes it is the only thing that *does* qualify us. It removes any pretense of self-reliance. Like a phoenix rising, we ascend from the ashes of our own undoing, testifying to the resurrecting power of God. From failure to forgiveness, weakness to strength, death to life—it's God's way. Remember that the next time you despair over your failures.

*I have pleaded in prayer for you, Simon, that your faith
should not fail. So when you have repented and turned
to me again, strengthen your brothers.* LUKE 22:32

DAY 36

☀ **A reflection on DEPENDENCE**
When I need to wait and trust

We must stop thinking of ourselves as the source of deliverance in a difficult situation. It is not up to us to save. Usually, we approach crises as though God is depending on us to do the work while He supports us in the background. We need to turn that around. We must depend on God to do the work while we are behind the scenes believing in Him. When He says to act, we must act. But most of us act far too quickly and believe much too slowly. We must be quick to believe and hesitant to interfere in God's work.

How do you react in a crisis? Do you feel responsible to step in and intervene? Perhaps God will require you to do so, but rarely until you have first trusted Him with a calm heart, sought His will diligently, made yourself fully available, and waited for His timing.

Jesus . . . said to the waves, "Silence! Be still!" Suddenly the wind stopped, and there was a great calm. Then he asked them, "Why are you afraid? Do you still have no faith?"
MARK 4:39-40

☼ A reflection on OUTWARD FOCUS
When I need to look beyond myself

Sometimes we can be outward-focused, seeing people's needs and trying to meet them. More often, we are just trying to get through the day, feeding ourselves and our families, and trying to earn enough to pay the bills.

Jesus urges His disciples to look beyond themselves. He tells them to thrive on the will of God and His passion for people who need the gospel. They are to be outward-focused, filled with vision. Their ambition should be to see the gathering of the Kingdom of God, not just to get through the daily grind. The substance of life is eternal, and we can invest it either in the Kingdom or in the world. Jesus points us to His Kingdom.

Do you understand why we are here? Do not be distracted by the daily routine or by the needs of the hour. Learn to recognize moments for sharing the gospel. Jesus has given us a mission and told us to have a vision for what's going on around us. Focus outward, not inward.

Wake up and look around. The fields are already ripe for harvest. JOHN 4:35

DAY 38

☸ A reflection on MONEY
When I need to address the materialism in my life

There is false worship in every human heart, and Jesus knows that all of it has some component of wealth. We either seek wealth and materialism as an idol in itself, or we have other idols that we cannot support without more money (approval of others, achievement, education, lifestyles, hobbies, food, fashion, and so forth). Almost any idol we can conceive of revolves around money as its object or for its sustenance. And when we harbor such idols, the Kingdom of God is like the eye of a needle to us. We just can't fit.

What idols grip your heart? Whatever they are, cut off their supply. They are fed by wealth, and they consume the Kingdom's resources, giving nothing of substance in return. Salvation is a matter of the heart, not the bank account. But if we are to live as Kingdom citizens, we must turn our hearts toward Kingdom purposes. Our wealth, our time, our abilities—all resources God has given us— must be invested in lasting goals. Our treasure will be where our heart is. And our hearts are in the Kingdom.

Jesus looked around and said to his disciples, "How hard it is for the rich to enter the Kingdom of God!" MARK 10:23

☼ A reflection on EVANGELISM
When I want to share God's heart for the lost

Anytime the Bible gives a name for God, we can know that it describes His character. When Jesus calls God "the Lord of the harvest," He is not describing something peripheral to God's identity. Bringing new believers into the Kingdom is at the very core of God's heart; it is who He is by nature.

Have you struggled with God's will for your life? Have you questioned where He would have you invest your energy? Whatever He has you do, you can be sure of this: reaching out to unbelievers will be an integral part of your relationship with Him. It is impossible to know the Lord of the harvest well without getting involved at some point with the harvest itself.

Perhaps your involvement begins where this verse does—with the asking. The first step in God's work is prayer. And rather than telling His disciples to pray for converts, Jesus' instruction is first to pray for workers. This is one of Jesus' most direct commands, and if we want to follow Him well, we will obey it.

The harvest is plentiful, but the workers are few. Ask the Lord of the harvest, therefore, to send out workers into his harvest field. LUKE 10:2, NIV

☀ A reflection on TRAGEDY
When I need an eternal perspective on death

In this world, people die. Survivors mourn. And we all think about the coming day when we will slip away from this visible world to whatever lies beyond. As Christians, we know what lies beyond, yet even we are shocked when this world is rocked.

Jesus points to the real issue—the eternal tragedy that many die without acknowledging their need for the Savior. This tragedy far outstrips anything this world can dish out. The consequences are infinitely more profound—not just a funeral service but eternal isolation from God and true life. There is no resurrection, no rebuilding, no reprieve in an eternity without Christ. It is forever.

We need to view life and death—and our neighbors—with an eternal perspective. We must understand that physical death separates us from those we love for a short time, but death without Christ separates those we love from the Presence of God forever. May a passion for God and an awareness of eternal realities compel us to live and to preach the gospel. Speak about it to someone today.

There is joy in the presence of God's angels when even one sinner repents. LUKE 15:10

DAY 41

☼ A reflection on CONVICTION
When the Holy Spirit reveals my sin to me

Having been saved by grace, we often still seek to be per-
fected by works. The Spirit will not let us. Although we
may have come to the Savior for forgiveness long ago,
God's Spirit will compel us to come to Him again today.
And tomorrow. And the next day. As long as sin is present,
the Spirit will continue to convict. Remember your need
of grace. Let your belief in Jesus' salvation be as real as it
was on day one.

When he comes, he will convict the world of its sin.
JOHN 16:8

DAY 42

☼ A reflection on THE HOLY SPIRIT
When I need to remember that the Spirit is active

A popular catchphrase asks us, "What would Jesus do?"
A better question is, "What is Jesus doing?" The first question makes Jesus a dead example. The second recognizes
His living Presence. The Holy Spirit shows us how to
live—not just in principle or by example, but in our actual
circumstances. The Spirit convicts us regarding righteousness because we need His righteousness to live in us. And
our world desperately needs to see Him. Let them see Him
through you.

*When he comes, he will convict the world of its sin, and of
God's righteousness.* JOHN 16:8

DAY 43

☼ **A reflection on DEATH**
  When I am afraid of dying

In many places in the world, Christians are put to death for no other reason than their faith. This is no surprise; Jesus said it would be so. According to recent statistics, Christians are the most persecuted religious group in the world. Still, there is something comforting in Jesus' words: "Not a hair of your head will perish!" He has just told the disciples that some will die, yet not a hair of their head will perish. How can this be?

Jesus doesn't define death as genuine harm. As frightening as death is to most of us, and as tragic as early death seems to us, we can all expect to die. Death is a universal experience, whether we are being persecuted for our faith or our bodies fail us for some other reason. Yet Jesus assures us that if we stand firm with Him (Luke 21:19), not a hair will perish. No real harm will come to us, because death for those who are in Christ is not real harm.

They will even kill some of you. . . . But not a hair of your head will perish! LUKE 21:16, 18

DAY 44

☼ A reflection on FAITH
When I want to trust God's power

Our inclination is to pray that God will move our mountains—according to our wisdom—so that we can see Him as able and willing. In His mercy, He sometimes answers. But God's inclination is to reverse the order. He wants us to see Him as able and willing before we pray. Then we will see mountains move—according to His wisdom.

Are there issues that overwhelm you? Relax and rejoice! God is teaching you an invaluable lesson about Himself. If you are crushed under the burden, He has you in a good place. He will drive us to this place whenever our problems are large and He is small in our eyes. He will let us be defeated so that we'll have no choice but to turn our eyes toward Him. He will let us come to the end of our own abilities so that we will see Him as so large that everything else becomes small. Faith precedes experience.

I tell you the truth, if you had faith even as small as a mustard seed, you could say to this mountain, "Move from here to there," and it would move. Nothing would be impossible. MATTHEW 17:20

☼ A reflection on FAITH
When I want to believe in God's power

When Jesus healed two blind men, He told them the healing was happening because of their faith. This statement is discomforting because we don't want so much to depend on our level of faith. But it can also be liberating when we realize that sometimes the only hindrance to our prayers is our faith. All we must do is grow in faith, and then God will act.

We must ask God to increase our faith. This is how a father appealed to Jesus when his son was suffering (Mark 9:24), and Jesus honored his request. We must also base our faith in God on something other than our own experience. The Bible is the answer. Meditate on the psalms and praises of the Word. Worship God for His goodness, His love, His power, His protection, and more. Saturate your life in His praise, and God will grow huge in your own eyes. And when He is huge, huge things happen—according to your faith.

Faith is nothing in itself. It's the object of our faith that matters. You want big faith? Worship a big God. The rest comes naturally.

He touched their eyes and said, "Because of your faith, it will happen." MATTHEW 9:29

☀ A reflection on FEARING GOD
When I wonder why it is wise to fear Him

Why does a God of love tell us that wisdom begins when we fear Him? Because when we approach the Holy One with a casual familiarity, we do not take Him as seriously as we ought, and we do not take our sin as seriously as we ought. Fear—not of punishment but of the overwhelming greatness of God—sees Him correctly. When this fear grips us, we begin to understand the enormity of the gospel and of our God. That understanding begins to rearrange our lives. And that is what wisdom is all about.

It is vital that we know God's love and rest comfortably in it. But a true understanding of God's love begins with an overwhelming awareness of His greatness, holiness, and power as they contrast our own sinful nature. This will shape our self-awareness, our relationships, our work, our prayers—*everything* we think and do. It will make us wise.

Fear of the LORD is the foundation of wisdom. Knowledge of the Holy One results in good judgment. PROVERBS 9:10

☼ A reflection on HEAVEN
When I need to satisfy my longing for eternity

God placed an impulse deep in our hearts for the things of heaven. He shaped us for eternity, and somewhere deep within us, we know that. In the meantime, we try to satisfy our hearts with things that don't measure up. That's why we always want more, no matter how much we have. Everything we think will satisfy us won't—not in the long run. Eternal impulses are not content with temporal treasures.

Where have you sought to secure your heaven? Even if you've placed your hope in the Kingdom of God, you still may be tempted to secure your kingdom by your own means. Have you insulated yourself in the most comfortable neighborhood, padded your bank accounts with the most comfortable margins, or gotten away from it all with the most comfortable respites? You may have cultivated your own parallel false kingdom next to the eternal Kingdom of God.

Resist that urge. God has called us into a relationship with Him, so let that be your treasure. Handle the things of this world loosely. Look for heaven where heaven really is.

We grow weary in our present bodies, and we long to put on our heavenly bodies like new clothing.

2 CORINTHIANS 5:2

DAY 48

☼ **A reflection on TIME**
When I need to rethink my priorities

Time is scarce, and the relentless clock will not slow down for us. In all of our juggling of families, jobs, church, and the rest, do we leave time for service? Does God get the very best of our time and of our effort? Are we just focused on getting things done, or are we wanting to help build an eternal Kingdom? How we spend our time and our effort will show us, the world, and God what our priorities are.

If a soldier demands that you carry his gear for a mile, carry it two miles. MATTHEW 5:41

DAY 49

☼ **A reflection on GOD'S HEART**
When I want to follow God's character

God is holy, and we must conform to His holiness. This means restrictions on our behavior. But when the restraints become the essence of our faith, as they did for the Pharisees, we are far from the heart of God. Faith in Him is not primarily about restrictions; those are just useful tools. Faith is about following His character. That's the whole point of obedience. It's an issue of our heart—and His.

Does the law permit good deeds on the Sabbath, or is it a day for doing evil? Is this a day to save life or to destroy it? MARK 3:4

☀ **A reflection on NEEDS**
When I wonder if God will take care of me

We tend to see our needs as either too large to ask even God to handle or too small for Him to be concerned with. But we are forgetful. We must be reminded of the God of history. He is the Provider who clothes the lilies and who sustained an entire generation with water and food in a barren wilderness. Too small for God to address? He is the God of five loaves and two fish. Too large? He is the Creator and Sustainer of all that is—is anything too difficult for Him?

What is your need? Whatever it is, it is entirely God's concern. He may instruct you in it, and the obedience is yours to carry out; but the provision is His. Let neither the enemy nor your own limited vision talk you out of dependence on Him. No need is too small, and none is too large. He is the God of compassion and the God of abundance, and best of all, He is our Father.

Jesus took the five loaves and two fish, looked up toward heaven, and blessed them. Then, breaking the loaves into pieces, he gave the bread to the disciples, who distributed it to the people. They all ate as much as they wanted.
MATTHEW 14:19-20

☼ A reflection on MY HEART

When I want my heart to be inscribed with love and faithfulness

In Deuteronomy 6, God told the Israelites first to love Him with all their heart, soul, and strength. Then He told them to take the words of the Law, divinely inscribed on tablets of stone, and inscribe them into the fabric of their souls. Let them be always on your hearts, He commanded.

Do you consider your heart to be a tablet? What is written on it? Do you realize that some things can be erased by the power of God and others inscribed by that same power? It requires your full cooperation, but the junk that we've inscribed there—through all of the media and entertainment we absorb, the relationships we've had, the information we consume—can be rewritten. It can be replaced with love and faithfulness. In fact, it *must* be replaced with love and faithfulness if we are to learn the mind of our God at all. This is who He is, and He insists that we become like Him. Love and faithfulness define Him. Do they define you? Let them saturate your heart.

Let love and faithfulness never leave you; bind them around your neck, write them on the tablet of your heart.

PROVERBS 3:3, NIV

☼ A reflection on THE LOST
When I think of those who don't know God

Sometimes we have a hard time understanding why others don't see the truth and receive the gospel like we did. But when we think this way, we are forgetful of our own sinfulness and ignorant of the Word of God. Wisdom, knowledge, and understanding come from Him. We do not earn it, nor do we discover it on our own. If He had not spoken it and opened our hearts to it, we would be like billions of others on this planet—living in total darkness. Pure grace gave us the truth.

This is a comfort to those of us who have loved ones who reject the gospel. The key to their understanding is not our convincing words or our clear explanations. Our most effective approach, to be supplemented by proclaiming the message and demonstrating love, is to pray that He would open their eyes as He has opened ours—by His unsearchable, unfathomable grace.

God is the consummate persuader. Do you know someone who needs the gospel? Pray—diligently, persistently, repeatedly. Pray that God will open eyes and hearts to His wisdom.

For the LORD grants wisdom! From his mouth come knowledge and understanding. PROVERBS 2:6

☼ A reflection on LOVE
When I want to answer Jesus' call to love

Most of us are conditioned to love those who will return the sentiment. But in the Kingdom of Heaven, love is not a sentiment; it's a choice. The *agape* kind of love that Jesus compels us to have for others cannot be answered with an "I don't feel like it." Feeling isn't the issue. The issue is whether we will live according to our citizenship in this Kingdom of God.

The culture of the Kingdom is shaped by its King. If He loved us while we were yet sinners, we must love others while they are yet sinners. The King's rules are different from everything our culture tells us is standard.

Do you have a standard sort of love? Jesus' calling is much higher than that. His calling means a radical departure from all the norms we once knew. It means divorcing the ways of this world and embracing a purer love. Not many people will travel with us on this road we've taken. But it is a journey definitely worth taking!

Love your enemies! Do good to them. Lend to them without expecting to be repaid. Then . . . you will truly be acting as children of the Most High. LUKE 6:35

DAY 54

☼ **A reflection on BLESSING**
When I want to receive God's full approval

The Bible is full of promises that God will bless His people. He is, by nature, an extravagant giver. It is not selfish to ask His blessing according to His nature. In fact, it is expected. But many of God's blessings carry prerequisites, and we forget them easily. We ask God for His favor, but we neglect the conditions on which He has already promised it.

Does God's blessing seem to be far from you? First realize that you have already been blessed, and be thankful. Then examine His Word. There are conditions that will carry further blessing when fulfilled. Obedience is one of them (Luke 11:28). So is godly character (Matthew 5:3-10). And humble service never goes unrewarded by the One who sees in secret.

The Master served His disciples. We are not greater than He is; we must be servants too. In so doing, we will bless others, and He will bless us in return. Those who give themselves to service in Jesus' name will receive God's favor. It is an inviolable spiritual law.

Now that you know these things, God will bless you for doing them. JOHN 13:17

DAY 55

☼ **A reflection on EMPTINESS**
   When I long for God

If our hearts are empty, they are empty only of God. He is the only real substance that can satisfy our cravings for fulfillment. Why do we press on after other things? Because we have bought into the lies of the evil one. Any discontent, any ache, any emptiness should drive us to our knees in hunger for God, which He promises to fulfill. Let's seek Him in every situation, turning to the truth that sets us free.

When [Satan] lies, it is consistent with his character; for he is a liar and the father of lies. JOHN 8:44

DAY 56

☼ **A reflection on CULTURE**
   When I don't feel a part of this world

Have you felt discouraged when there is friction between you and this world because of your identity in Christ? The clash of cultures between the Kingdom of God and the kingdom of this world can be frustrating. But let it encourage you. Remember that it is a sign of your foreign citizenship, evidence of your relationship with the eternal Son of God. Rejoice that your relationship with Him is taking precedence over your relationship with the world.

The world would love you as one of its own if you belonged to it, but you are no longer part of the world.
JOHN 15:19

DAY 57

☼ **A reflection on TRANSFORMATION**
When I want to have a renewed mind

What should the renewed mind of the believer look like? When we are transformed, we will begin to understand our time, our treasures, and our talents differently. We will stand in a dramatically different place than we once stood, and our perspective will reflect the change. Our eyes will gaze on new heights, and our desires will lean in new directions. We are a new creation; we will learn to live as one.

If you have lost sight of the radical nature of the new mind or the constant call of the new creation, let your mind be transformed and your life be renewed again and again. It is a lifelong process for the believer, a work that God will complete the day He takes you into His Presence. Never settle for the status quo. And never lose sight of the upward call of God out of the ways of this world and into the heart of His will.

Don't copy the behavior and customs of this world, but let God transform you into a new person by changing the way you think. Then you will learn to know God's will for you, which is good and pleasing and perfect. ROMANS 12:2

☀ A reflection on FOLLOWING JESUS
When I want to grow in discipleship

Following Jesus is not about living a religion; it's about knowing a living Person. He didn't just leave us a legacy of teachings, He left us Himself. We don't get our marching orders from Him and then proceed to live the Christian life without Him. We don't observe and applaud His words and His works from a distance without getting into the game ourselves. We don't base our discipleship on our feelings, which come and go as often as the wind changes direction. We follow.

The promise of discipleship is that we are not alone in our obedience. We are following a Person. We can talk with Him, cry with Him, listen to Him, and work with Him. Unlike many religions that teach their adherents a set of principles and then send them out to live those principles, the living Jesus is with us as He teaches us. We *should* have principles, feelings, curiosity, and reasons, but we do not base our lives on any of these alone. We follow *Him*.

"Follow me and be my disciple," Jesus said. LUKE 5:27

☼ A reflection on STRUGGLE
When I wonder why life is so difficult

If life has been a struggle, there's a reason. The Kingdom of God that you crave is in conflict with the fallen world that you live in. You have welcomed the new while surrounded by the old. That does not make for a peaceful life. In fact, the Christian life is impossible unless there's a new birth, a constant faith, a learned dependence, and a holy ambition. Knowing the Holy Spirit is essential. Otherwise we are simply fallen creatures striving and wishing for something better.

Don't be discouraged by the fact that there is a battle in your life. The battle, in fact—if it is between the new and the old, the true and the false, or the gospel and the world—is evidence that you are a citizen of the Kingdom of God.

The battle also comes with a promise: we are ransomed unharmed. It may not seem like we're unharmed, but by God's definition, we most certainly are. There is no enemy stronger than He "who has ruled forever" (Psalm 55:19). Your Savior reigns. Remember that when the battle rages.

He ransoms me and keeps me safe from the battle waged against me, though many still oppose me. PSALM 55:18

☼ A reflection on FAITHFULNESS
When I need to be loyal in small acts of service

We tend to think that accomplishing something in God's Kingdom means building large ministries with an extended reach. We are impressed by those who have impacted lots of people in highly visible ways. But even these things began small. God's Kingdom is a mustard-seed kind of enterprise. Huge ministries often begin with one small step of faith. Lives are often changed by one kind word. Hearts are touched by one soft song, or one frightened witness, or a cup of cold water given in His name. Nothing in His Kingdom is too small to count—or even too small to grow into something huge.

Never despise the small things in your life. Never spend so much time reaching for the high-impact acts of ministry that you neglect the minute details of service. The massive doors of God's Kingdom swing on tiny hinges of our faith and obedience. Focus on the hinges, and you'll see the doors open wide.

Jesus said, "How can I describe the Kingdom of God? . . . It is like a mustard seed planted in the ground. It is the smallest of all seeds, but it becomes the largest of all garden plants."
MARK 4:30-32

DAY 61

☼ A reflection on FREEDOM
When I feel enslaved by sin

As Christians, we know we have been freed from the penalty of sin, but often we still feel enslaved by it. We know we have eternal life, but how often we feel imprisoned in a body of death! We can easily feel trapped in mundane, uneventful lives. We are so frequently stuffed back into our shackles that the excitement of our freedom seems a distant memory.

Focus today on Christ as Deliverer. Think of what robs you of your joy in Christ and makes you feel imprisoned. Know that whatever it is—whether it is within your heart or some external constraint—Christ is victor over it. Consider how an imprisoned Paul and Silas sang joyful hymns to God and how a dying Stephen saw heaven opened. None were bound by their surroundings. What binds you? Circumstances? Discouragement? Sin? Ask God to reopen your eyes to Jesus the Liberator.

He has sent me to proclaim that captives will be released, that the blind will see, that the oppressed will be set free.
LUKE 4:18

DAY 62

☼ **A reflection on TIME**
When I need to establish priorities

When our time is unfairly demanded of us, how do we respond? Jesus does not ask us to be doormats. He asks us to be witnesses. We are the display of His Kingdom's truths. If tasks are a greater priority to us than relationships, how will this world see His values? God asks us to take a stand for Kingdom principles. We must decide which is more important to us: protecting our precious time, or demonstrating the Kingdom of God.

If a soldier demands that you carry his gear for a mile, carry it two miles. MATTHEW 5:41

DAY 63

☼ **A reflection on TRUTH**
When I feel caught in my circumstances

Our human tendency is to feel trapped by visible situations. But circumstantial evidence is deceptive. God's assessment is always the truth of every situation. Are circumstances threatening what you know to be God's plan? They lie. God's plan, when believed, is immovable. Those who focus on their problems find those problems to be overwhelming. Those who focus on Jesus find their problems to be illusory. Focus on Jesus.

He told them plainly, "Lazarus is dead. And for your sakes, I'm glad I wasn't there, for now you will really believe. Come, let's go see him." JOHN 11:14-15

☼ A reflection on PATIENCE
When I am waiting on God

Patience is one of the hardest virtues for us to understand. We pray to an omnipotent God. We know He is able to help us at any moment. We know that He who defines Himself as "love" and gave His Son for us is not reluctant to help us. So when we ask such a God to intervene in our circumstances, why is there so often a delay?

God has His reasons. Perhaps our needs are being prolonged because they are accomplishing something in us that nothing else will. Perhaps they are being prolonged because God is doing a necessary work in the life of someone else who is involved in our situation. Perhaps He is teaching us about prayer or perfecting our faith. The Christian's wise response is to know that if we are waiting on God, there must be a very good reason. And if we wait in faith and expectancy, the wait will be amply rewarded. His timing is always perfect.

I waited patiently for the LORD to help me, and he turned to me and heard my cry. PSALM 40:1

☼ A reflection on WORDS
When I want to bless others with what I say

Positive words have power. A good word can edify. It can confirm the talents, the skills—even the life direction—of someone who only needed a little encouragement to keep going.

Not only can our mouths bless others, they can also draw attention to the glory of God. They can tell of His great works, witness to His unfathomable mercy, and marvel at His remarkable ways. In fact, our mouths were created entirely for such purposes. The tongue was given to bless others and to bless God. In so doing, it will bless us as well.

Have you failed to use this potent source of blessing? If negative words come out of your mouth, reverse the trend. Use your mouth to bless at all times. You will find the current of your life to flow in a corresponding direction. When blessing comes out of your heart, God makes sure that blessing comes into it. Release your tongue to do what it was meant to do.

Sometimes [the tongue] praises our Lord and Father, and sometimes it curses those who have been made in the image of God. . . . Surely, my brothers and sisters, this is not right!
JAMES 3:9-10

☼ A reflection on GLORIFYING GOD
When I want to be a witness through my trials

We can become extremely self-absorbed in a trial. We see how it will impact us, we pray for deliverance from it, and we obsess about how to work ourselves out of it. But we often become blind to God's larger purpose. Our trials, though they seem like disasters to us, may be God's means for bringing honor to His name. We are to seek His glory in all circumstances, even the ones that pain us deeply. They are often His means of letting the world know who He is.

How does Jesus display Himself in our trials? That depends on our response. Are we in a situation where people are trying to compel us to conform to the world's standards? Then Jesus is displayed in our refusal to be conformed. Are we suffering in a way that would cause most people to despair or cry out in bitterness and anger? Then Jesus is displayed as we demonstrate that this world's travails are swallowed up in our hope of eternal life. Whatever we go through, it can result in our being witnesses.

This will be your opportunity to tell them about me.
LUKE 21:13

DAY 67

⚙ **A reflection on THE END TIMES**
When I need to be ready for the future

Right after Jesus tells His disciples to watch for signs and to recognize them, to see and to know when the time of His coming is near, He tells them that He will come when they do not expect Him. What a curious mix of clarity and mystery! There will be signs and we should expect Him, but no one knows the day or the hour. What is Jesus trying to accomplish with so much teaching yet so little certainty?

Jesus wants us to be on guard. He wants us to be able to tell, generally speaking, what events signal the end. He has given us signs because He wants us to be ready. But He has given us ambiguous signs because He wants *every* generation to be ready. Readiness and a watchful eye are always the appropriate pose of the believer, in all times and in all places. Because of Jesus' words, the expectation has been building throughout church history. That is exactly how He wants it. We are to wait and to watch—and to be ready at any time.

You also must be ready all the time, for the Son of Man will come when least expected. MATTHEW 24:44

DAY 68

☼ **A reflection on GOD'S WAYS**
   When I want to follow His direction for my life

When Proverbs 4:26 commands us to make level paths and to take firm ways, it is not telling us to follow conventional wisdom. This is not a suggestion to play it safe. It is an order to follow God, to heed His wisdom and trust His guidance, no matter how foolish it looks to a skeptical and watching world. It is a call to base our lives in the ultimate reality of Scripture rather than in the finite understanding of human logic. We must understand that the level and firm paths are the ones that are level and firm in God's sight—not ours, not anyone else's.

When you seek direction for your life, give no attention to whether your path is safe or risky, conventional or unconventional. Consider only whether it is based in God's truth, sensitive to His voice, and reflecting His purposes as revealed in His Word. This is ultimately the only safe, level, firm way there is.

Make level paths for your feet and take only ways that are firm. PROVERBS 4:26, NIV

DAY 69

☼ **A reflection on THE FUTURE**
When I need to look ahead to Jesus' return

Are we ready for Jesus' return? If we are living according to our past, we are not. But if we are living according to our future as fellow heirs with Christ and children of the living God, then we can know that we are ready. Let your future guide your present. Remember who you are in Christ and who He promises you will be for all eternity. Know that He is coming again and your future will be fulfilled.

Anyone who belongs to Christ has become a new
person. The old life is gone; a new life has begun!
2 CORINTHIANS 5:17

DAY 70

☼ **A reflection on PRAYER**
When I feel alone

If ever we feel weak or alone in the work to which God has called us, we can turn to John 17 and read Jesus' prayer. It is a prayer for us—for all believers—and the Son of God does not have unanswered prayers. His will is one with the Father's, and His prayers are accomplished. Dwell on this encouraging thought: if you belong to the Father through faith in the Son, the Son is praying for you even now.

My prayer is not for the world, but for those you have given
me, because they belong to you. JOHN 17:9

⚙ A reflection on UNITY
When I consider the power of God's name

The name of God is the holiest and most sacred of all words, especially in the Jewish context of Jesus' ministry. There is an inexpressible reverence for His name that exists because of the awesome power of the Person it invokes. There is nothing more mysterious, more feared, more awe-inspiring than the name of the living, eternal God.

Jesus' request for the unity of His disciples is backed by the power of His name. This is no casual request. The name of God solemnly seals this unity. It is done.

The unity of true believers has never really been at stake in all of church history. What has been at stake is whether we behave as if we are united. We *are* one in Christ—that is reality. Do we *act* as one in Christ? Pray that our churches would reflect the spiritual reality of the body of believers. And then live with that oneness in mind.

Holy Father, you have given me your name; now protect them by the power of your name so that they will be united just as we are. JOHN 17:11

☀ **A reflection on JOY**
When I want to find deep contentment

There is no doubt in God's revealed Word that tremendous joy is on His agenda for us. And yet how many of us fail to experience that joy! Is it the trials that come to us? Do our own failures convince us that we are outside of the gospel of joy? Jesus' words give us the answer to how we can experience joy in our circumstances: "Here on earth you will have many trials and sorrows. But take heart, because I have overcome the world" (John 16:33).

Does joy elude you today? If so, set your gaze on the Christ who has overcome the world. The Savior who lives within you is the same Savior who went through ultimate hardship and gave us a firm hope above and beyond it. His promises are abundant, and they are real. He does not offer us joy without a concrete basis for it. Count on it, rest in Him, and experience His joy in full measure.

I told them many things while I was with them in this world so they would be filled with my joy. I have given them your word. JOHN 17:13-14

☼ A reflection on PURPOSE
When I wonder if my life has any point

We exist to appreciate God's glory—there is no higher purpose for us. It is no wonder, then, at the end of Jesus' earthly ministry, that He prays for us to see His glory. But the amazing thing is that Jesus also wants us to share His glory by *having* some of it (John 17:22). Unworthy as we are, He has given us the glory that the Father gave Him. In beholding His glory, we are able to reflect it (2 Corinthians 3:18). What a privilege!

We often feel trapped in mundane lives—just existing rather than actually living with purpose. Jesus' prayer reminds us that our purpose far exceeds our ability to even begin to comprehend. We are partakers in the glory of God. We were created to see it. We were created to enjoy it. And we were created to share it with Him. Trapped in a meaningless existence? Never. We are children of God. Share His glory.

Father, I want these whom you have given me to be with me where I am. Then they can see all the glory you gave me because you loved me even before the world began!
JOHN 17:24

☼ A reflection on PRIORITIES
When I am too focused on the here and now

Jesus knows our tendency to focus on making a home for ourselves. Try this little exercise: compare, on the one hand, the amount of time we spend with our eyes focused on getting an education, earning a living, establishing a career, building a home, staying healthy, and achieving our goals; and on the other hand, the amount of time we spend with our eyes focused on our Master and His mission. For most of us, the scale falls clearly on the side of the things of this world.

Yet which is more important? Our answer to that defines whether or not we are disciples. Not that the elements of each option are always incompatible—it isn't wrong to earn a living, build a home, or stay healthy. Jesus' followers just cannot make priorities of those endeavors. When we do, our lives are out of order.

Jesus replied, "Foxes have dens to live in, and birds have nests, but the Son of Man has no place even to lay his head."
LUKE 9:58

☼ A reflection on STEADFASTNESS
When I want to remain faithful in worship

One thing God looks for when we are in the crucible is a steadfast heart—a heart that will not, under any circumstances, fall away. God will sometimes wait to answer our cries until it is clear to Him, to us, and to those who observe us that our heart is resolutely fixed on Him. And more than just steadfastness of hope is required; it is a steadfastness of worship, too. The heart that learns to make music in its darkest moments is the heart that is delivered.

The deliverance usually comes twice. First, a worshipful heart can find deep joy regardless of what's happening on the outside. Second, a resolved, singing heart then finds deliverance in a God who responds. God does not remain silent in His love when we do not remain silent in our worship.

When circumstances oppress, the battle rages, and the heat of the crucible rises, where is your heart? Is it steadfast in its worship? If so, expect deliverance within and without. You can sing your song of victory before victory even comes. In the most important sense, it already has.

My heart is confident in you, O God; my heart is confident. No wonder I can sing your praises! PSALM 57:7

DAY 76

☀ A reflection on LIVING FAITH
When I need to remember that Jesus still speaks today

The Bible is the backbone of our faith, but we tend to read it historically, as though Jesus is only an ancient teacher and not a living Lord. He will *never* contradict His Word, but the Word is not just a memory preserved. Jesus is alive. He continues to teach. He still disciples us and leads us. When you read the Bible, do you hear the words of a risen Savior?

There is so much more I want to tell you, but you can't bear it now. When the Spirit of truth comes, he will guide you into all truth. JOHN 16:12-13

DAY 77

☀ A reflection on WORSHIP
When I want to enjoy God wholeheartedly

Do you want the Presence of God to be revealed in your life in a powerful way? Worship Him from your heart, not just your lips. Read your Bible with a passion for His fellowship. Sing your congregational songs while meditating on each word. Fellowship with other believers with a thankfulness for the Spirit that works in and through them. The warm, welcoming Presence of God will be as real as the praises of your heart.

Sing psalms and hymns and spiritual songs to God with thankful hearts. COLOSSIANS 3:16

☀ A reflection on GOD'S NATURE
When I want to change my instinct to get even

Have you ever thought about our natural reaction when people offend us? Our first gut feeling in such cases is to respond in kind, to return ill will for ill will, to rise to the same level of spite with which we've been treated. Somehow, we must reverse that impulse. We must learn to think of mercy first. But how can we alter something that is so ingrained?

The key is to ask the question that's really underneath the others: how can we be more like God? God told Moses that He is "the God of compassion and mercy! I am slow to anger and filled with unfailing love and faithfulness. I lavish unfailing love to a thousand generations. I forgive iniquity, rebellion, and sin" (Exodus 34:6-7). How can we be more like that?

We have two options: We can try to reform the sinful human nature, or we can ask God for His nature. The former approach has never in history proven successful. Our only remaining option is to ask God. He offers us His nature. We must ask and believe He will give it. He always does.

God blesses those who are merciful, for they will be shown mercy. MATTHEW 5:7

☼ A reflection on CONDEMNATION
When I am tempted to judge others

Christians have earned a reputation for condemning others. Some of this is simply that we stand up for what is right, but some of our reputation is warranted. We often wrap up within our proclamation of truth an indictment of those who don't live up to it. But Jesus never asked us to condemn—and He Himself said He did not come to condemn.

We must ask ourselves: Does our mission match the message of Jesus? In proclaiming the gospel to the world, are we hard on self-righteousness but merciful toward sinners? If not, we are not like Him, and we must question how much we have let His words and His life saturate our minds. In trying to do the work of the Holy Spirit by convicting the world of sin, we may be demonstrating mistrust that God will do as He said. It is His responsibility to convict of sin. The *only* gospel Jesus sends us into the world to preach is truly good news: forgiveness of sins by the abundant grace of God to all who believe.

God did not send his Son into the world to condemn the world, but to save the world through him. Whoever believes in him is not condemned. JOHN 3:17-18, NIV

※ A reflection on REPUTATION
*When I am striving to make a good impression
on others*

In Jesus' code of ethics, there is no room for an inflated
sense of dignity. That isn't to say that we have no dignity;
created in the image of God, we could have no less. What
Jesus prohibits is our instinct to defend our "approval
rating" in others' eyes. We are not to guard our image as
though our self-esteem depends on people.

Why are we so concerned about the impression we
make on others? And why are we so convinced that a vigor-
ous defense of our rights makes a better impression than
our humility? Jesus articulates what ought to be clear to us:
Honor comes to those who do not strive for it. The most
admired are the most humble. The Kingdom of God is
well represented not by the strident and the overassertive,
but by those who know their heavenly citizenship and
are entirely content with it. That's how we can become
unattached to our reputation; we already know who we are.

*You have heard the law that says the punishment must
match the injury: "An eye for an eye, and a tooth for a
tooth." But I say, do not resist an evil person! If someone
slaps you on the right cheek, offer the other cheek also.*
MATTHEW 5:38-39

☼ A reflection on REST
When I need to pursue quiet time with Jesus

The person who does not get alone with Jesus is sure to have difficulty as a disciple. This getting away is essential; there can be no growth or genuine service without it. That's because it is in the quiet places that Jesus refreshes us. Jesus did not tell His disciples to get away for a change of pace. He told them to come with Him. His Presence is the difference between a temporary rest and a lasting refreshment.

In the quiet places, Jesus gives us rest. He also teaches us how to depend on Him more fully, how to serve Him more effectively, and how to trust Him more implicitly. The quiet places are places of growth. We deepen our fellowship with Him, and instead of a temporary rest, we have a relationship that will continue to sustain us when the pressures of life are on us again. The things we learn in the calm with Him today are the things that will help us survive in the storms ahead.

[Jesus said,] "Come with me by yourselves to a quiet place and get some rest." MARK 6:31, NIV

⚙️ **A reflection on REST**
When I am burdened

When Jesus tells us to take His yoke—the piece that binds and guides a beast of burden—upon us, He is not telling us to leave a state of freedom for His captivity. We are already slaves to our sense of independence and self-management. No, when He offers us His yoke, He is offering us a way out of the self-effort we've insisted on for years. He is offering us life-giving direction and purpose. He is generously giving us His own life. Dependence on Jesus is a prerequisite for obedience. We cannot reverse the order without being crushed beneath the obligations of life and our attempts at self-righteousness. We must be taught dependence first.

There is a huge difference between a taskmaster and a teacher. Which way do you most often view Jesus? Learn to see His yoke as a life-giving promise. Though He insists on everything we have in the transaction, He demands it for our freedom, not our captivity. Remember the gentleness of your Teacher, and know that His yoke *never* adds to your burden.

Take my yoke upon you. Let me teach you, because I am humble and gentle at heart, and you will find rest for your souls. MATTHEW 11:29

☀ **A reflection on BOLDNESS**
When I want to be light in a dark world

This world seeks answers but condemns anyone who claims to have them. It honors openness to all kinds of "truths" but scoffs when one accepts *the* truth. But our Master has given us neither a light to be hidden nor a spirit of fear. The world craves answers, and though it does not recognize Him, He is the answer. We have no apologies to make for offering the light of salvation to a world in darkness. Be bold.

You are the light of the world—like a city on a hilltop that cannot be hidden. MATTHEW 5:14

DAY 84

☀ **A reflection on DISCIPLESHIP**
When I want to leave everything behind to follow Jesus

The greatest adventure a person can have is to follow Jesus without hindrances. When we try to pick up the trappings of our old life to carry with us, we soon find out that we follow at too great a distance. Jesus urges us onward, calling us to leave all behind and focus our eyes entirely on Him. He calls us to a new way of life.

"Follow me and be my disciple," Jesus said to him. So Levi got up, left everything, and followed him. LUKE 5:27-28

☼ A reflection on THE HOLY SPIRIT
When I am searching for guidance

The things we often crave the most from the Holy Spirit are His direction and His power. We want to know which relationships He wants us to focus on, which career direction to take, and which area of service to perform. But the Holy Spirit has higher priorities for us than the ones for which we usually beseech Him. First and foremost He wants to give us the guidance and power to be holy—to be sanctified. He wants to bring to life the cleansing words of Jesus and make the Kingdom of God the treasure of our hearts.

Have you sought special guidance from the Holy Spirit? Is there some act of service, area of ministry, or life decision that occupies your thoughts? Perhaps the Holy Spirit wants to meet you there but has a prior item on His agenda. He wants first things first. Let Him have His way. Let Him saturate you with Jesus' words and ways so that you will be made in His likeness. Make His holiness your first pursuit. Then God will be glorified in everything you do.

[Jesus said,] "The Spirit will tell you whatever he receives from me." JOHN 16:15

☼ A reflection on CHARACTER
When I want my life to reflect God's nature

The one who has meditated on the life and law of God will be firmly established. He or she will be like a tree planted by streams of water. And there *will* be fruit. There's no doubt about it: when the season is right, fruit will come, and the fruit will be good. Why? Because there is an infinitely rich, ever-flowing stream of water that nourishes this tree. It is not a tree that establishes itself; it is planted and tended by the living God.

He calls us to be like Himself. His eternal character produced the purity of the Law, words of wisdom, the voices of the prophets, the saving work of Jesus, and the life of the church. What does our character produce? If it comes from God, it produces reflections of the very same themes. It produces the kind of prosperity that glorifies God and keeps us in His extravagant grace. It produces fruit that lasts forever.

They are like trees planted along the riverbank, bearing fruit each season. Their leaves never wither, and they prosper in all they do. PSALM 1:3

☼ A reflection on SERVANTHOOD
When I need to take on Christ's attitude

Our churches and ministries often resemble worldly institutions with their power structures, self-interest, and man-made methods. But the body of Christ is to be radically different. It is to be the one body on earth that subverts the fallen order. It is to be characterized by servanthood and humility.

Jesus modeled this for us in a number of ways: ministering to outcasts, washing the disciples' feet, and most significant, dying for our sins. Yet despite the divine example, we often act in ways contrary to the Master. We are more like the disciples who argued about who was the greatest. Our attitudes reflect an unwillingness to be like Jesus, no matter how often we might call Him "Lord."

"You must have the same attitude that Christ Jesus had," Paul says (Philippians 2:5), before describing the humility of Christ. Christians who are characterized by that attitude glorify Him and demonstrate that they are not of this world.

Those who are the greatest among you should take the lowest rank, and the leader should be like a servant. . . . For I am among you as one who serves. LUKE 22:26-27

☼ A reflection on UNANSWERED PRAYER
When I want to respond with faith

Often God's initial answer to us after a prayer is not His final word; it is a test. It is given to see how we will respond. Is it a response of faith and trust? Or a response of complaint? The nature of the reply may determine the result we see. We will either honor Him with a confident declaration of His merciful nature or we will dishonor Him with resentment and resignation. In either case, He may or may not give us the answer we hoped for. But when we respond in faith, He *will* answer, one way or another. It is inconceivable that He would ignore those who fall at His feet and pray to Him in faith and on His terms.

How do you respond when Jesus doesn't answer the way you expect? Do you turn away in bitterness? That's certainly not what He wants. His desire is to see us profess our knowledge of who He is, even when the superficial evidence we see seems to contradict His true nature. He welcomes persistence, He expects faith, and He sympathizes with those who know their desperate need.

Keep on knocking, and the door will be opened to you.
LUKE 11:9

❋ A reflection on THE CROSS
When I need to remember that God is available

Most Christians believe at some level that God is unknowable. It is true that we can never know everything there is to know about Him. But He has made Himself known through the Cross. There He is Judge and Redeemer, wrath and love, holy and merciful, mighty and wise. Everything we will ever need was made available there.

Need salvation? It is given to us on the basis of Jesus' blood and the power of His resurrection. Need wisdom? It is freely given at the Cross too. Need anything at all from God? He calls us to meet Him there—every time, for every purpose.

Never underestimate the availability of God. God invites us into the victory of the Cross and the resurrected life that follows—to know it, to savor it, and to tell it. Never cry out to God, "Where are You?" without looking first at the Cross. Understand what He has freely given and base your life on it. At the Cross, His wisdom is yours.

We have received God's Spirit (not the world's spirit), so we can know the wonderful things God has freely given us.

I CORINTHIANS 2:12

DAY 90

☼ A reflection on TAKING UP MY CROSS
When I need to let go of my pride

Jesus says: "Take up your cross *daily*." Not once at our first glimpse of Calvary. Not occasionally when we feel a need to repent. Daily. If we live by pride daily, we must undo pride daily. And nothing undoes pride but the Cross. It reminds us that our remedy is not simply to try to do better, but to die to ourselves and be resurrected with Christ. The Cross is our model for living for Him.

If any of you wants to be my follower, you must turn from your selfish ways, take up your cross daily, and follow me.
LUKE 9:23

DAY 91

☼ A reflection on THE CROSS
When I need to follow Christ more closely

When we read of Jesus' crucifixion, we see the pain of self-denial. But we forget—the Cross was also the path to ultimate fulfillment and glory. It was so for Jesus, and it is so for us. The cost looks overwhelming at first glance, but there is ultimate liberation beyond it. It's the liberation of surrender to a wiser, gentler, more powerful Lord than the one we're accustomed to—ourselves. We can find freedom by embracing this Cross.

If any of you wants to be my follower, you must turn from your selfish ways, take up your cross, and follow me.
MATTHEW 16:24

⚜ A reflection on JESUS' PRESENCE
When I can't sense Jesus with me

Mary and Joseph were perhaps given history's most sacred charge: parenting the Son of God. And they lost Him! For more than three excruciating days, He was missing. They looked among their traveling companions. They searched all over Jerusalem. When they finally found Him, He calmly reassured them: Where else would He be? The Temple is His home.

Don't we also search for Jesus? Even though we are assured of His Presence, He often seems awfully absent. Yet Jesus does not leave us to despair. What greater commitment could He make than this: "Didn't you know that I must be in my Father's house?"

We do not need to wonder where He is. He is always about His Father's business, which is dwelling in and working out His plan in believers. In light of the post-Resurrection fact that our bodies are His temple—both individually and corporately—what greater assurance of His Presence can He give? His own nature compels Him. He *must* be in His Father's house, and His Father's house is us.

[Jesus said,] "Didn't you know that I must be in my Father's house?" LUKE 2:49

☼ A reflection on THE GOOD SHEPHERD
When I need God's heart for the lost

Jesus says that He is the Good Shepherd. And in Matthew 18, Jesus tells us that the Shepherd is zealously focused on restoring lost sheep. Our God is a seeking God. He will gladly leave behind the ninety-nine in their comfort and safety in order to track down a single misguided sheep. All heaven rejoices when that sheep is found (Luke 15:7, 10).

Do we want to align ourselves with God's plan? Then we must single-mindedly pray for those who are lost. We must work to find them and to bring them into the Good Shepherd's fold. We must give our resources toward this end. God does not rest as long as there are lost sheep, and neither can we.

Today there are more than four billion sheep outside the Shepherd's fold. If we want to be in tune with God's priorities, we must pray, give, train, tell, send, go—and never rest—as long as sheep are outside the fold.

If a man has a hundred sheep and one of them wanders away, what will he do? Won't he leave the ninety-nine others on the hills and go out to search for the one that is lost?
MATTHEW 18:12

☼ A reflection on SECURITY
When I need to remember the reliability of God's Word

Jesus points us to the priority of His Word. It is what will keep us from deception, and it is what we can cling to when heaven and earth seem uncertain and the end of the age seems near. There is nothing transitory about Jesus' words. If we fasten ourselves to what He says, we are bound to Jesus Himself. And if we are bound to Him, we have nothing to worry about when the heavens and the earth seem unstable.

There is a deep sense of security that comes from knowing that the words of Jesus are a permanent reality. They are not confined to the world as we know it; even if time itself were to come to an end, His words would not. They do not fail us.

If you invest your whole self in Jesus' teaching, letting it saturate your mind and sink to the depths of your heart, you will have a profound knowledge of your security in an uncertain age. Do you want that? It's His open invitation.

Heaven and earth will disappear, but my words will never disappear. MARK 13:31

⚙ A reflection on WORRY
When I wonder what my anxiety says about how I view God

Consider what our worry says of our opinion of God. When we stress and strain over a situation, are we affirming His providence and abundance? Are we embracing His grace? No, our anxiety reveals our mistrust of God's sovereignty; it is an emotional slander of His character. We may justify our worry by observing all of the tragedies in the world around us, knowing that such may befall us as well. Yet God promises His sovereignty even over these, as well as His Presence with us in the midst of them.

Dare we suggest by our worry that some catastrophe may slip by without His notice? No, "tragedies" befell Joseph, Moses, David, Jesus, Paul, and others, and God ordained them all for good. All of these surely could have worried, examining their circumstances while going through them. But looking back, we see God's perfect plan unfolding. Therefore God urges, even commands: do not worry.

That is why I tell you not to worry about everyday life— whether you have enough food and drink, or enough clothes to wear. Isn't life more than food, and your body more than clothing? MATTHEW 6:25

☀ A reflection on SERVICE
When I wonder how best to help others

What is true servanthood? Many mistake it for slavery—being on call for the whims and pleasures of another. Biblical servanthood is different. It actively seeks the true well-being of others. Just as Jesus served His disciples and us in a completely unexpected way—dying for sins rather than overthrowing our earthly enemies—we are called to do what's best for others. Serving others should deepen their relationship with God and demonstrate grace.

Do we spend our days looking for those whom we might serve? Probably not. Our own agendas become so large and consuming that we rarely depart from them, at least not without feeling inconvenienced. Yet servanthood is integral to the gospel. Nowhere else does Jesus give us a path to greatness. Need an illustration? Think of a life that began in a lowly stable and ended in human sacrifice for the sins of the world. It was servanthood from beginning to end. And no greater life was ever lived.

Whoever wants to be a leader among you must be your servant. MATTHEW 20:26

☀ A reflection on GOD'S PRESENCE
When I want to be more aware of God with me

How can we know God's Presence? By love and obedience—two sides of the same coin. To obey Him is to love Him, and to love Him is to know His Presence in a deeper, fuller way. The people who are most aware of God's Presence are the ones who love Jesus with a passion and who have abandoned all disobedience to Him. God uses them without reservation. May we each strive toward this goal.

All who love me will do what I say. My Father will love them, and we will come and make our home with each of them. JOHN 14:23

DAY 98

☀ A reflection on BECOMING LIKE GOD
When I need to know more of God's character

As God's children, we are called to be like Him. Whom God loves, we are also to love. Those impurities in ourselves that God despises, we are also to despise. His way is to become our way. Study God's character in Scripture. Examine His tenderness and compassion, His holiness, His hatred of evil, and His love. As we see Him as our standard, let us also see the radical transformation that must take place as we grow to be like Him.

The Lord—who is the Spirit—makes us more and more like him as we are changed into his glorious image.
2 CORINTHIANS 3:18

☸ A reflection on RESURRECTION
When I am reminded of the truth that Jesus is alive

Death surrounds us. It is on our TVs and in our newspapers. It has taken family members and friends. It will come to each of us. Yet for all who are crushed by the reality of the Fall, Jesus gives this promise: there is a resurrection.

Perhaps we have heard this so often that we have lost a sense of amazement over this impossible claim. But think about it. This just does not happen! Most religions have some concept of an afterlife, but a man being physically raised from the dead? No one ever made such a claim—except Jesus. It's beyond the realm of possibility. People die and they are buried. Period.

But Jesus erased the period. His resurrection, far from being an exclusive privilege of the Son of God, means everything for us. It reversed the curse of death that we brought upon ourselves at the Fall. It is the re-genesis—the beginning of a new creation. And we are invited to be a part of it.

The Son of Man is going to be betrayed into the hands of his enemies. He will be killed, but three days later he will rise from the dead. MARK 9:31

❀ A reflection on NEW LIFE
When I want to live in the truth of the Resurrection

The life that we live by faith is an exchanged life—everything that we were went with Jesus on the cross; everything that He is was raised from the tomb and is given to us. We gave up everything in our old nature to have that substitute on the cross. In return, we gained the life of the everlasting Son of the living God, with all of His privileges and power. What an exchange!

The only sad thing about this exchange is that we are forgetful creatures. Having accepted the Cross as our payment for sin, we forget to live in the Resurrection that follows. Our old natures remind us of what we were before the Cross. And we listen.

Yet Jesus is the Resurrection and the Life. He offers to fill us with His glorified self. The substitution of the Cross is not just in death, but in resurrection. We may now live in the power that raised Him—but only if we live by faith. Are you living that life? Or better yet, is He living that life in you? Believe in the Resurrection and the Life.

Jesus told her, "I am the resurrection and the life. Anyone who believes in me will live, even after dying."
JOHN 11:25

☀ A reflection on GRACE
When I am humbled by a recognition of my sin

Grace begins with a crisis. It cannot be understood apart from a clear recognition that we need it desperately. When we hear the truth about ourselves, as Paul did on the road to Damascus, we should be humbled. The revelation of our true nature and the fact that we were all once enemies of God (Romans 5:10) would be psychologically devastating if not for the grace that follows. Jesus speaks the painful truth. And sometimes that truth is incredibly humbling.

God means for us to walk in this kind of humility. No redeemed people are spared from the knowledge of their offenses before God, because it is only in that knowledge that we can stand in His grace. It is harsh, yes, but behind the harshness is the love that brings us to Him. Is there any pride in the way we Christians relate to God or to one another? Let it be undone by the severity of truth and the comfort of grace.

He fell to the ground and heard a voice saying to him, "Saul! Saul! Why are you persecuting me?" "Who are you, lord?" Saul asked. And the voice replied, "I am Jesus, the one you are persecuting!" ACTS 9:4-5

⚙ **A reflection on PEACE**
When I need to remember that Jesus has overcome the world

Seeds are buried in the ground. Caterpillars are confined in a cocoon. Grain is pummeled into flour. But each one has a higher purpose and either another world to experience or a function to fulfill. So do we. We can easily make the mistake of thinking that God's primary purpose for us is a matter of our lifetime on earth, while His heavenly Kingdom is an afterthought. But the Kingdom is the main event. Like the seeds, the caterpillars, and the grain, we are in an elemental form, being shaped by the Father for greater, lasting purpose.

The world is the arena in which we are trained. As God shapes us for His Kingdom, He uses many means. One of them is the tribulation that our world naturally dishes out. But our trouble is not meaningless; we can take heart. Peace is found in seeing beyond the training ground that so often distresses us. It is found in placing all hopes in the One who overcomes the world.

Here on earth you will have many trials and sorrows.
But take heart, because I have overcome the world.
JOHN 16:33

☼ A reflection on LOVING GOD
When I need to rekindle my devotion to God

Many have observed that if the greatest commandment is to love God with all of one's heart, soul, mind, and strength, then the greatest sin of all is to fail at this commandment. But who among us has kept it for even a few minutes? The one thing we were created for—a deep, abiding, consuming love for God—eludes us while we busy ourselves with avoiding greed, pride, lust, anger, impatience, and a host of other sinful traits. We spend our energy fighting symptoms when the ultimate source of our sickness is a loveless heart toward God.

True discipleship is an outgrowth of love for Him. After years of trying to follow in Jesus' steps, we may discover that He values our affections even more than our works, for only out of the former do the latter flow. To have our love for Him revived is to experience ultimate joy. Ask God to kindle in your heart an abiding love for Him.

You must love the LORD your God with all your heart,
all your soul, all your mind, and all your strength.
MARK 12:30

☼ A reflection on RESOURCES
When I want to invest in eternity

What do you do with what God gives you? All He gives is for one primary purpose—building the eternal Kingdom. Wherever we prove faithful in building that Kingdom, we will be given ample resources, increasing with our measure of generosity. Wherever we prove unfaithful, we'll find ourselves empty—perhaps not now, but eventually. Examine your investments, direct them toward eternity, and expect God to make them fruitful.

Whoever has will be given more; whoever does not have, even what they have will be taken from them.
MARK 4:25, NIV

DAY 105

☼ A reflection on SACRIFICE
When I wonder about the cost of discipleship

If you believe you are walking as a disciple, and there seems to be no sacrifice in your discipleship, check again. Somewhere, you are missing His voice. There is always an element of cost. God accepts only the best of our resources. As living sacrifices (Romans 12:1), our offerings will cost us dearly—the very best of who we are. But they also bring us blessing—the very best of who He is.

If any of you wants to be my follower, you must turn from your selfish ways, take up your cross, and follow me.
MARK 8:34

☀ A reflection on GRACE
When I need to extend kindness to those around me

God showed up on our planet in the form of a merciful Savior. He offers grace without rebuke to those who know they need it. His rebukes are saved for those who won't acknowledge their need. He is purity that pursues the corrupt; mercy that hounds the needy; grace that demands only belief.

"All of us who have had that veil removed can see and reflect the glory of the Lord. And the Lord—who is the Spirit—makes us more and more like him as we are changed into his glorious image" (2 Corinthians 3:18). Let us meditate on how well the Savior's character is becoming a part of our lives. As we are conformed to His image, we should see in ourselves the characteristics that He displayed. We should sit at the table with "tax collectors and sinners" with their need for healing in mind.

Are we like Him? Do we have extravagant mercy? When people describe us, does their description reflect in some small way His winsome call? May our attitude be, "I am here for sinners."

I have come to call not those who think they are righteous, but those who know they are sinners. MATTHEW 9:13

☼ A reflection on COMMITMENT
When I want to value the gospel above all else

Jesus told a parable about a merchant discovering a very valuable pearl. There are several ways to approach this parable. One of them is to understand Christ as the pearl and us lost human beings as the searching merchants. The implication is that when the gospel comes into a person's life, it is *everything*. It is not a philosophy to add to the mix, or an access to God that will help us accomplish our goals. It is a radical rearrangement of all of life.

Is Jesus *everything* to us? Or one loyalty among several? If someone asked us how much we would give up in order to know Him, is there anything we would hold back? Do we believe only when it doesn't cost us too much? It's easy to know the right answer to these questions; a wholehearted abandonment to Christ is more difficult and more profound. What is the pearl of your life?

The Kingdom of Heaven is like a merchant on the lookout for choice pearls. When he discovered a pearl of great value, he sold everything he owned and bought it!
MATTHEW 13:45-46

☀ A reflection on ATTITUDE
When I need to serve out of love and gratitude

With service in the Kingdom of God, attitude is everything. What attitudes are behind our gifts? What attitudes are pleasing to God?

We often think we have fulfilled God's requirements in our service for Him. We can easily be satisfied with fulfilling our duties, but God much prefers acts of love to acts of duty. Even if we gave 90 percent of our income, our time, and our effort for the Kingdom of God, it would not be enough for Jesus if there were no love in it. It may be better to fulfill our responsibilities as Christians than not to fulfill them at all; but the Kingdom of God is not primarily about fulfilling responsibilities. It is more about expressing gratitude and about being passionate for His glory.

When we bring God our offerings—whatever they are—we must come with a genuine desire to give them. We must offer them because we love God and we desire to see His Kingdom come. And we must give them in thankfulness that He, by example, knows a lot about lovingly giving it all.

I tell you the truth, this poor widow has given more than all the others who are making contributions. MARK 12:43

☀ A reflection on LOVING OTHERS
When I need to develop the heart of a shepherd

Just as the question in John 21:17—"Do you love me?"—reminds us of the great commandment to love God with everything that is in us, the imperative of the verse—"Feed my sheep"—reminds us that there is a second great commandment to love our neighbors as ourselves. To have a heart for God is also to have a heart for that which concerns Him. And God has made it known throughout Scripture that He is passionately concerned for His people. The Great Shepherd tends to His sheep. He watches them, He feeds them, He protects them. He cares more deeply than we can know.

Do we have the heart of a shepherd? Are we passionate about the welfare of others? Do we tend to one another with the same concern with which the Great Shepherd tends to us? Too often we envision our love for God as a separate endeavor from our love for others. But the two are intertwined. The first, if genuine, inevitably leads to the second. To love God is to love our brother.

[Jesus] asked him, "Simon son of John, do you love me? . . . Then feed my sheep." JOHN 21:17

DAY 110

☀ A reflection on FRUITFULNESS
When I want my actions to line up with what I believe

How do we detect false teachers? Jesus' answer is simple: it's all in the fruit. When we hear a new teaching, of course we listen closely to the teacher's words to determine if they line up with our understanding of biblical doctrine. But an even better indicator is the behavior of the teacher. If we really want to know what people believe, we will not focus on their words but on their actions.

We can apply Jesus' principle of fruit to ourselves as well. What we do will indicate what we believe deep down inside. If we say we believe in the power of prayer but rarely pray, we don't really believe what we say. If we say we believe in the power of love to change lives, yet harbor critical and judgmental attitudes, once again we deceive ourselves. Our deeds contradict our words.

What is the evidence of genuine belief? Learn to discern the truth. It's all in the fruit.

Yes, just as you can identify a tree by its fruit, so you can identify people by their actions. MATTHEW 7:20

DAY 111

☀ A reflection on FEAR
When I am afraid

What threatens you? Are you feeling out of control? Perhaps the elements have frightened you out of your wits. Don't worry. Jesus is the absolute authority over everything in your life, if you will trust Him with it. There is perfect timing in His commands, and your storm will not linger a moment too long. Learn that when you are with Him, every threat is a false one.

When Jesus woke up, he rebuked the wind and said to the waves, "Silence! Be still!" Suddenly the wind stopped, and there was a great calm. MARK 4:39

DAY 112

☀ A reflection on FELLOWSHIP WITH CHRIST
When I want Jesus to make his home in my heart

We don't need to clean ourselves up entirely for Jesus before He comes into our lives. But we do need to be prepared—and willing—for *Him* to do a thorough cleaning. He's not just at our door for a visit; He's moving in. But Jesus is mostly here for the fellowship; He wants to sit at the table and enjoy your company. If you want that, tell Him how welcome He is.

Look! I stand at the door and knock. If you hear my voice and open the door, I will come in, and we will share a meal together as friends. REVELATION 3:20

DAY 113

☀ **A reflection on CARES**
When I need to cast my concerns on God

What does it mean to cast our cares on the Lord? It's the difference between being sustained and faltering, between faith and fear. If we're confused on this point, we will be riddled with anxieties and phobias, afraid to face the future and far from the will of God. If we understand, we can go through anything with peace in our hearts. When we cast our cares on Him—when we trust Him with our concerns—we ask Him to manage them.

We acknowledge our own futility, and we rely on His power to resolve them. We actively watch, not ignorantly wait. We expectantly believe, not aggressively intervene. We act when He says to act and sit still when He says to sit. We can go to sleep at night knowing we can do nothing more effective than acknowledging His wisdom, power, love, and lordship. We can wake up without a single burden, because our burdens are on His shoulders. We refuse to micromanage. We will hope only in Him, because He is where our cares have been cast.

Cast your cares on the LORD and he will sustain you; he will never let the righteous fall. PSALM 55:22, NIV

☀ A reflection on GOD'S WILL
When I need to trust that the Father's plan is good for me

We know that we should pray for God's will to be done, but we're often afraid to. Why? Because we do not trust that His will is best for us. We think His agenda and ours are by nature at odds with one another.

Because of our corruption, they may in fact be at odds. But if we could see the whole picture, we would understand that it is our own will that falls short of fulfilling our well-being, not His. If we really understood, we would know that when His will and ours clash, His is by far the better of the two, not just for His own purposes, but also for our happiness and eternal blessing. If we could see as well as He does, we would choose His will over ours every time—not because we're mature, selfless, and God-centered, but even for our own self-interest. What He wants is always best for us.

May your will be done on earth, as it is in heaven.
MATTHEW 6:10

☼ A reflection on IDENTITY
When I consider what it means to belong to God

We are not our own. We belong to God. Isn't this easy to
forget? We tend to approach life with a certain autonomy,
as though we are independent individuals with a responsibility to acknowledge God in worship and sacrifice. But
God wants a deeper worship in our lives. Rather than living
independently of Him while giving Him our respect, He
wants us to live dependently on Him with awareness that
every action, every thought, every impulse is to fit into His
purposes. We must not act—or even breathe—without this
awareness. We have been bought. We are His.

And our Master is the epitome of benevolence. He
knows our innermost being and is zealously intent on fulfilling us. The Christian who lives with this wisdom—
that we are owned by Another—is a Christian profoundly
changed. Our decisions are affected, our character is
reformed, and our load is lightened. We lose the right to
ourselves, but we also lose the burden of self-rule. It is a
wonderfully freeing truth. Everything about us is the concern of Someone else.

*You do not belong to yourself, for God bought you with a
high price.* I CORINTHIANS 6:19-20

❂ A reflection on WORK
When I want to glorify God in my responsibilities

God has not placed us where we are simply for the output we can produce, whether it is at a factory, at a desk, at school, or at home with children. He has put us there because that is a context in which He wants to display Himself. Our work is about Him, even if it's entirely secular in our minds. We are there because God wants to put godliness on display for others to see. He wants to infiltrate the culture we work in.

Is godliness at work your preoccupation? If you're like many people, you may feel like your work is pointless, your boss is unfair, or your coworkers are petty. Never mind. None of those things are the point. The point is for the Holy Spirit to dwell in you there, wherever you happen to be. And in that sense, you are working for God, not for the one who signs your paycheck. Whatever you do, have this in mind: you are doing it not just because God wants you to be there, but because He wants to be there too.

Work willingly at whatever you do, as though you were working for the Lord rather than for people.
COLOSSIANS 3:23

※ A reflection on EMOTIONS
  When I want to walk by faith, not by sight

We fallen humans generally make decisions by sight, which often means that we let our emotions be our guide. We do what we want to do, and pride and feelings rule.

Of course, God created our emotions and He intends for them to be fulfilled, but He does not intend for them to rule us. If they did, our lives would be roller-coaster rides, moving up and down with every whim and trend. God transcends our feelings, and when we elevate them above His wisdom, we are placing ourselves on the throne of our own heart—where only He belongs.

God's prescription for our wisdom is to find His. His is constant; His is eternal; His is deeply rooted in reality— the way things *really* are. His wisdom is everything our emotions are not. A believer who forsakes his or her own feelings for the much more reliable guidance of the eternal God has become wise. Sight is limited; faith is not. We must walk by faith, not sight.

We live by faith, not by sight. 2 CORINTHIANS 5:7, NIV

DAY 118

☸ A reflection on CULTURE
When I am weary of going against the flow

As believers, we must swim upstream in the raging rapids. The unbelieving world is radically opposed to the gospel, and the gospel is radically opposed to it. Are you discouraged in this upstream journey? Be encouraged. We will fit perfectly in the coming Kingdom. And as we live by its principles, we will draw others into it.

Blessed are the poor in spirit, . . . those who mourn, . . . the meek, . . . those who hunger and thirst for righteousness, . . . the merciful, . . . the pure in heart, . . . the peacemakers, . . . those who are persecuted. MATTHEW 5:3-10, NIV

DAY 119

☸ A reflection on JUDGING
When I am tempted to criticize

Nowhere does Jesus tell us to be quiet about our society's moral ills. But we must take a stand from a position of identification with sinful humanity, not from a position of superiority over it. We are part of the problem. Those who judge others about immorality as if they are above it believe deep down that they have earned God's favor, and no one listens. But when we speak as sinners saved by grace, many will hear with open minds.

You will be treated as you treat others. The standard you use in judging is the standard by which you will be judged. MATTHEW 7:2

☀ A reflection on ABUNDANT LIFE
When I want to prevent Satan from stealing my joy

Satan's mission is to steal our joy, terminate our lives, and leave a legacy of devastation. He wants us to mistrust Jesus and start making decisions based on fear and anxiety. So we must resolutely fix our gaze on God and His Word, and remain unswerving in devotion to Jesus.

We must always remember Jesus' mission—giving us abundant life. It may not always be easy or comfortable, but it will be good and founded on His joy. When we are confident in God's will, and circumstances arise that seem to contradict His will, we must know where they come from and cling to God. If we let circumstances constrain us, Satan will manipulate them indefinitely, stringing us along our whole lives in uncertain, fear-induced steps.

Our faith must fix its gaze on Jesus and not waver. God's voice must be the only one we hear. It's the key to abundant life.

The thief's purpose is to steal and kill and destroy. My purpose is to give them a rich and satisfying life.
JOHN 10:10

☀ A reflection on CONFESSION
When I am afraid my sin will discredit the gospel

Much has been made of the possibility of people in the church bringing discredit to the gospel. The line of reasoning is this: The gospel cleanses us from sin. Therefore, when one of us falls into sin, the cleansing power of the gospel is discredited. But is this true? Does a sinning saint damage the gospel's reputation?

That depends. Someone who claims to be right with God, but who clearly is not, may weaken the witness of the message. But someone who falls, confesses, and repents—no matter how great the fall—only confirms the power of the truth. That person has demonstrated the meaning of grace.

Are you hiding your sin? The church often unwittingly encourages its members to do so. But *that* denies the gospel. Bringing it openly to the Cross exposes the sinner as sinful but also exposes the gospel as powerful. May we always know the freedom to live in the light.

Those who do what is right come to the light so others can see that they are doing what God wants. JOHN 3:21

DAY 122

⚙ A reflection on SPIRITUAL WARFARE
When I need to remain alert

We know life has its struggles, but we are often blissfully unaware that there is cosmic warfare going on around us, and it is always intense. We have been told to stay awake and keep watch, but we keep falling asleep.

Whether we like it or not, when we put our faith in Christ we left civilian life. We try to revert to a peacetime lifestyle whenever we can, but the attacks of the enemy have a way of reminding us where we are. We are on the battlefield, and though we know the outcome already, our opponent, Satan, forestalls his final defeat as long and as vengefully as he can.

That's why the New Testament emphasizes faith and prayer as much as it does. Faith is our weapon against the enemy, and prayer is our communication with the headquarters from which come all our resources. And until we have been called home to Jesus, His orders for us remain the same—stay here and keep watch.

Stay here and keep watch with me. MARK 14:34

☼ A reflection on THE POWER OF GOD
When I need to be reminded of God's supernatural ability

When we pray, do we hint that Jesus might not be able to do what we ask? That the circumstances might just be too overwhelming even for Him? Jesus would lovingly mock us with the same response He gave the father of a boy who needed to be healed: "What do you mean, 'If I can'?" Of course He can. His adequacy is not the question. And because no situation is bigger than He, neither is any prayer. Our requests should be huge. The issue for us is not whether He can, but knowing His will and His ways—and assuming the best of them.

Jesus may answer our prayers exactly the way we expect Him to—or He may not. But He *always* stands ready to intervene in response to our belief. *Never* does He refuse a persistent, patient, trusting plea for His involvement. He is always willing. And He always can.

"Have mercy on us and help us, if you can." "What do you mean, 'If I can'?" Jesus asked. "Anything is possible if a person believes." MARK 9:22-23

☀ A reflection on THE LIFE OF THE SPIRIT
When I want to be controlled by the Spirit

There are two options for the believer—the way of human nature and the way of the Spirit. Yet it is entirely possible for us to be born of the Spirit and to walk according to the flesh. Paul's pointed question to the Galatians is relevant to us: "After starting your Christian lives in the Spirit, why are you now trying to become perfect by your own human effort?" (Galatians 3:3).

God did not birth us by His Spirit in order for us to live in our own strength. There is a supernatural source readily available to us for our decisions, our ministry to others, the unity of our relationships, our worship of God, and more. We are so accustomed to our old nature that we forget to invite the power of God to live in us. Yet in the Kingdom of God, the all-sufficient Savior chooses to *be* our life rather than watch us struggle in our own strength. He inhabits His devotees, and if they will allow it, He'll demonstrate His Presence. Let Him. You were born for this.

Jesus replied, "I tell you the truth, unless you are born again, you cannot see the Kingdom of God." JOHN 3:3

DAY 125

☼ A reflection on PEACE
When I'm seeking security

We live in an unsettling world, so we fill ourselves with false securities. We surround ourselves with safety measures, especially those that protect our physical lives. But the world is fraught with hazards, not just physical, but also spiritual and emotional. Who can protect us? Real security can only be found in Christ. It does not matter what threatens us if we know He is with us. He has promised us peace. And His promises are certain.

The peace I give is a gift the world cannot give. So don't be troubled or afraid. JOHN 14:27

DAY 126

☼ A reflection on THE FOUNDATION
When I need to build my life on Christ

There are all types of houses in the world. Big and small, beautiful and plain, lavish and humble. Regardless of the style, the crucial question is the foundation underneath it. The same is true for our lives. Are Jesus' words the foundation for our work? For our attitudes? For our habits? For our use of time and money? For our relationships? If they are not, we build our houses in vain. If they are, whatever we build will be solid.

[Jesus said,] "Anyone who listens to my teaching and follows it is wise, like a person who builds a house on solid rock."
MATTHEW 7:24

☀ A reflection on WORSHIP
When I need renewed spiritual perspective

Worship is a learned art. It is an attitude of the heart that continually acknowledges God and values His character. It is the ultimate reflection of reality in the mind of the believer. And it is the key to blessing.

Worship gives us a new perspective, placing us in the realm of God's power, wisdom, and love—the realm of eternal truth. It opens the eyes to what is real. With natural eyes, we often see our struggles as huge obstacles and our chances of overcoming them as slim. We are easily overwhelmed. We know our limitations, and God's omnipotence seems distant. But when we worship Him, we shed those earthbound illusions. Our worship brings us into the light of His Presence and reminds us who He really is.

God's greatness makes all other things—especially the hard things—seem small. It allows us to pray with confidence and faith that we, through Him, will overcome. When He fills our hearts with His Presence, no burden can fill our hearts with its weight. Learn the art of worship, and be blessed.

Happy are those who hear the joyful call to worship,
for they will walk in the light of your presence, LORD.
PSALM 89:15

⚙ A reflection on JUSTICE
When I am anxious to see wrongs made right

God loves justice, and we who have been created in His image love to see things work out in a way that is fair for everyone. We hate inequity, especially when we're on the short end of the imbalance. Our sense of fairness is really rankled when God's timing does not equal our own. We know things will be made right at the judgment seat of Christ, but we want restitution *now*.

How do you make things right when you've been wronged? Revenge is not a biblical option; God insists that vengeance is His, not ours. And perfect fairness is not a biblical option either; we who have received a clean slate from our Savior can have no complaints against our God of justice. Justice once directed at us was poured out on Another, so we can hardly insist that others must receive it.

Does that bother you? Relax. God *will* make all things right, in His time and in His way. He is patiently waiting for all who will repent; a verdict now would be premature. Seek justice now, when appropriate, but don't place your hope in it. God's is worth waiting for.

Many seek the ruler's favor, but justice comes from the LORD.
PROVERBS 29:26

☼ A reflection on GENEROSITY

When I want to give to others what I have been given

We often hoard the gifts God has given us as our own possessions. They are not; they were given for a broader reason. He intends not only to care for us, but to care for us in such a way that we become like Him in our care for others. Those who have been forgiven are to forgive. Those who have had debts canceled are to cancel others' debts. Those who have been given ample resources are to be generous with them. Those who have been healed are to declare His healing. Whatever He has done for you, you are to do for others. It's that simple.

Jesus' blessing is the means for us to bless others. However we have experienced the Kingdom of Heaven, that's how we are to share it. Then, as we become His channels, we experience the nearness of the Kingdom—and the King.

Go and announce to them that the Kingdom of Heaven is near. Heal the sick, raise the dead, cure those with leprosy, and cast out demons. Give as freely as you have received!
MATTHEW 10:7-8

☼ **A reflection on LOVING OTHERS**
   When I want to care like Jesus does

Jesus knows our feeble efforts at love. It is no coincidence
that He commands us to love just as He does immediately
after His teaching on the branch's relationship to the vine.
Love is a form of bearing fruit, and Jesus is emphatic that
we can bear no fruit on our own (John 15:5). It is by our
abiding in Him, and by His abiding in us, that fruit happens. It is by the same union that love happens.

   If we attempt to love others as Jesus loves us, we will fail.
We can try to muster up feelings, but they will fall short.
We can try to love independently of our feelings, but it will
be a hollow, lifeless love. No, the only remedy is the living
Vine bearing fruit through His branches. He is the source.
Do you want greater love for others? Bask in His love, and
see what happens next.

*[Jesus said,] "Yes, I am the vine; you are the branches. Those
who remain in me, and I in them, will produce much fruit.
For apart from me you can do nothing. . . . This is my
commandment: Love each other in the same way I have
loved you."* JOHN 15:5, 12

☀ A reflection on REWARDS
When I wonder what I will gain from serving God

There is a false spirituality in the church that insists that
we are never to serve God with an eye on the reward. Yet
over and over again, Jesus uses reward as an incentive for
His disciples to follow Him at all costs. Jesus assures us
that even though the costs of discipleship are great, they
will never outweigh the benefits. We serve Him knowing that there is surpassing value in our service and in the
rewards we will reap from it. God is no one's debtor. He is
extravagant in His promises.

Jesus expects His disciples to leave *everything* behind.
But it's another of the many paradoxes of the gospel. In
losing everything, we gain everything *and more!* Though
we invest much of our lives in houses, property, and relationships with friends and relatives—all good things—the
gospel is of inestimably greater worth. The gospel, if we
accept it, will loosen our grip on all our attachments while
making our attachment to Christ supreme. The cost of that
is huge, but the reward is greater still.

*Everyone who has given up houses or brothers or sisters or
father or mother or children or property, for my sake, will
receive a hundred times as much in return and will inherit
eternal life.* MATTHEW 19:29

DAY 132

☀ **A reflection on SIN**
When I am struggling with recurring lapses

Many Christians struggle with habitual sin. It has power—from the world, our own flesh, and the evil one. And that power is intense. We are to forsake it, but only Christ can break its power (Romans 7:25). If this is your struggle, cry out to Him and don't stop asking until He does. And know that He will. He is stronger than the thief, and His will is that we have life in all its fullness.

The thief's purpose is to steal and kill and destroy. My purpose is to give them a rich and satisfying life.
JOHN 10:10

DAY 133

☀ **A reflection on WORRY**
When I am too concerned about what will not last

Worry occurs when we've overvalued something that is corruptible. Possessions, opportunities, health, relationships, jobs, and all else we need for daily existence are important, but they are not essential to our life in Christ. We often hold them too dear, and they become our idols. When they are threatened, our hearts are troubled. But if we fix our hearts on Jesus, we find rest. He is our Refuge, our Shield, and our Provider. And He can be trusted.

Don't let your hearts be troubled. JOHN 14:1

☼ A reflection on GOD'S AUTHORITY
When I need to remember that God is sovereign

There is no greater authority, not in this world or any other. Our universe is governed by the Son of God, the Ancient of Days incarnate, the Alpha and the Omega. Whatever impresses us, frightens us, threatens us, embitters us, or thrills us—all that we can imagine and more—is under His reign. He is the ultimate power.

That's great, we might think. But what does it have to do with us? The answer is glorious. This infinite power, ultimate authority, and King above all kings is the very same One who intercedes for us. He is on our side. And if the ultimate authority intercedes for us, who will overturn His intercession?

The greatest power in all the universe—*over* all the universe, in fact—is already inclined toward us, dedicated to working out our good, and available through our prayers. We might not notice such support if we are bent on our own agenda, but if we are bent on His, there is no obstacle that can obscure it.

Jesus came and told his disciples, "I have been given all authority in heaven and on earth." MATTHEW 28:18

☼ A reflection on COMPASSION
When I need to care more deeply for others

In Jesus, we see the compassion of an infinite God in the heart of a human body. What an overflow of emotion! We are amazed at the implications of boundless love incarnate.

What is really amazing about Jesus' compassion is that His emotions are also expressed through us when His Spirit reigns in our hearts. We have access to a love beyond ourselves. When we come across the really unlovable, we may ask Him to love them through us. When our human nature recoils at the offensiveness of others, we may trust the Holy Spirit to minister to them in spite of our own impulses.

Jesus' compassion reaches into lepers' wounds. It goes to the side of the road where victims lie. It sees needs and seeks to meet them. It welcomes offensive prodigals back home. If Jesus is love incarnate, and His Spirit is in us, we will love with His kind of compassion. This compassion will come from beyond ourselves. All we have to do is ask Him for it.

When he saw the crowds, he had compassion on them because they were confused and helpless, like sheep without a shepherd. MATTHEW 9:36

☀ A reflection on EYES
When I want to fix my attention on Jesus

Many sins begin with the eyes. What the eyes gaze upon, the heart begins to crave. They can lead us to holy cravings for God and truth, but they also lead us in paths of coveting and lust. A glimpse turns into a gaze, a gaze turns into a craving, a craving turns the heart aside, and a misdirected heart wreaks havoc on godliness and service.

Take an inventory of what you stare at. The results will tell you a lot about what is important to you. In all likelihood, you will find some things that are inappropriately significant to you and that fall short of God's good will for us.

A tendency to look aside indicates dissatisfaction with what you already have. If you are dissatisfied, the answer is not in looking in new directions; it is in strengthening your gaze on the Savior and His ways. Fix your eyes on what is ultimately worthy of your attention. Gaze at Jesus.

Look straight ahead, and fix your eyes on what lies before you.
PROVERBS 4:25

DAY 137

✳ A reflection on DISCERNMENT
When I need to guard against spiritual temptations

The nuances of our temptations have a way of making the wrong decisions look right—even appealing. That's why a spiritual life without vigilance is incredibly irrational. If we are not watchful and well guarded, we can be led step by tiny step into the snares of the enemy and the ways of the world. What *seems* right and what *is* right are often two vastly different things.

As Christians, we will face many forks in the road throughout our lives and often will not even notice them. The main road—the broad, well-traveled path—seems like the right one. Everyone is on it, and the exits are often hard to see unless you're looking for them.

So look for them! Don't be driven down the seemingly right path without asking hard questions about it. Understand the high call of the Kingdom—that God has us do more than what's right, more than what's expected. Let His Word cultivate a sharp discernment in your spirit. Never let yourself be seduced by anything but the good love of God.

There is a path before each person that seems right, but it ends in death. PROVERBS 16:25

☼ A reflection on AMBITION
When I want to follow God's recipe for greatness

We human beings are too often caught in a misguided ambition—toward self-fulfillment, toward achievement, toward impressive accomplishments, and toward status. The problem with our ambition is that it strives toward unworthy goals. It misses what is truly valuable. It exalts self to the exclusion of God.

Contrary to our instincts, God's means for greatness are not climbing up the ladder, but going down. Why? Because when our ambition accomplishes much, we get glory and we compete with God. When our ambition rests in what God can do, He gets glory. That's why He came as an infant in an obscure little town. He is more clearly the author of greatness when the great get such lowly starts.

Do you desire greatness in God's Kingdom? It's not a bad desire. But the means may not be what you'd expect. Measure greatness not by status but by dependence on the One who is greater than all others.

Anyone who welcomes a little child like this on my behalf welcomes me, and anyone who welcomes me also welcomes my Father who sent me. Whoever is the least among you is the greatest. LUKE 9:48

DAY 139

☼ **A reflection on WORSHIP**
   When I need to put my relationship with God first

We often elevate our work for Jesus—like feeding the poor—above the Person of Jesus. When we do, we subvert the proper order. Our values are distorted, and our works become empty. Worship is to come first. It is paramount. There is no praise too lavish for Jesus. He is the highest priority, ultimately valuable above all other concerns. Do you want to reflect true worth? Let your work flow out of a heart enamored with Him.

[Jesus said,] "You will always have the poor among you, but you will not always have me." JOHN 12:8

DAY 140

☼ **A reflection on WAITING FOR GOD**
   When God seems silent

Children learn much about their friends by playing hide-and-seek. They don't give up when they can't find them at first; they keep looking. In a similar way, might God's silence—which we experience sometimes when we pray—prepare us for an encounter with Him? God often does not answer us immediately, but He encourages our persistence. He invites us in the silence to explore His character and learn of His will. He tells us to seek and we will find.

To everyone who knocks, the door will be opened.
LUKE 11:10

☀ A reflection on GOD'S AGENDA
When I want to find meaning for my life

In the vastness of creation, we begin to glimpse the height, depth, and breadth of the power of God. Incredibly, that's the same power that is working within us to conform us to His image. It is also the same power that sends us out to accomplish His agenda. And what is that agenda? He makes it plain: make disciples of all peoples, baptizing them and teaching them (Matthew 28:19-20). The highest goal of God is to be worshiped—*everywhere*.

What a sacred charge! If ever we wondered what God wanted us to be busy with, this is it. After Jesus' declaration that all authority in heaven and on earth is His, He tells us where His authority is directed. It has one remaining goal: restoring the rebellious race back into the pure image of God.

Do we want meaning in our lives? *Here it is.* Do we want to know we are in God's plan? *This is it.* Do we want to know power? *This* is the mission that has "all authority" behind it.

Jesus came and told his disciples, "I have been given all authority in heaven and on earth. Therefore, go and make disciples of all the nations." MATTHEW 28:18-19

☼ A reflection on CARING FOR THE LOST
When I need to tell others about Jesus

Think of the odd assortment of people to whom Jesus was drawn. A dishonest tax collector, a prostitute, an adulteress, beggars, lepers, and just about everyone else who had no legitimate case to make about their own righteousness and well-being. They knew they needed help.

If our identity is in Jesus, and His Spirit is living in us, we will be drawn to others as He was. We will be brokenhearted about those who suffer in sinful, diseased conditions just as He was—and is—brokenhearted. Our zeal to bring His redemption into a captive world will in some way reflect His zeal. It will be a diagnostic measure of the reality of our union with Him.

The knee-jerk reaction to the imperative of seeking and saving the lost is to try to cultivate a desire to do so. Resist the urge. Be aware of the need, but respond by cultivating your union with Jesus. You cannot muster up the appropriate zeal, but fellowship with His Spirit will make His agenda contagious to you and those around you. Let His mission become yours.

The Son of Man came to seek and save those who are lost.
LUKE 19:10

☼ A reflection on MOTIVES
When I want to bring glory to God, not to myself

Many people do their acts of righteousness in order to bring praise to themselves. It's a hollow righteousness that may earn compliments and status, but it's nothing that God will honor. Truly righteous acts come from hearts that seek God's glory—and God's glory should never be hidden. Those who do good works with a right heart never point to themselves. They point to God, and are glad to do so. Their works cause others to marvel at God's grace and power, not a human being's goodness.

It's a constant temptation to do things for our own glory. We must examine our motives for the good things we do. Do we seek God's glory? Are we realistic enough to know that anything good coming out of our lives comes from His grace and mercy and not from our own purity or ingenuity? The rewards of heaven are reserved for those who are background players to the glory of God. We must magnify others' view of Him without drawing attention to ourselves.

Don't do your good deeds publicly, to be admired by others, for you will lose the reward from your Father in heaven.
MATTHEW 6:1

☀ A reflection on INVESTING IN THE KINGDOM
When I want to devote myself to what will last

In the economy of God, one investment is clearly superior to all others. It's a sure thing. And Jesus calls us to place all of our resources, time, and talents there—exclusively. Why? Because He knows the return it will yield, and He knows we will not be disappointed. But there is often a part of us that wants to diversify. We want to invest some in God's Kingdom, certainly, but also some in this world. We're afraid to put our resources in only one place.

Human beings pursue comfort and pleasure with great passion. It isn't that comfort and pleasure are wrong; God created both for us to enjoy. But He never called us to pursue them. To the contrary, He constantly calls His disciples to take everything they have now and invest it in everything they know about God's eternal Kingdom. Consider your investments well, and avoid the pursuits of this world. Whatever you do, do it for the glory of God.

What do you benefit if you gain the whole world but lose your own soul? MARK 8:36

☼ A reflection on WORRY
When I am anxious about material things

When we're worried, friends often tell us, "Don't worry. It will be okay." But our friends can really do nothing to change a stressful situation other than be with us as we walk through it. Jesus can do more than this. If *He* is in a position to tell us not to worry, it must mean that His Father is aware of our needs and our future, and able to do something about them both.

God feeds and clothes His children. No one who trusts in Him is abandoned by Him. His children may go through hardship; they may even die—but never before He specifically allows it in His own timing. Never is their provision beyond His purview.

Above our worries is an active Provider with a perfect sense of timing. He is in control, even when we aren't sure how tomorrow's needs will be met. When we run after provision, we are running after the wrong thing, something that God has claimed as His domain. We are to run after His Kingdom and righteousness. That's what we were made for.

That is why I tell you not to worry about everyday life. . . .
Seek the Kingdom of God above all else, and live righteously,
and he will give you everything you need.
MATTHEW 6:25, 33

DAY 146

⚙ A reflection on BLESSING OTHERS
When I want to pay forward God's gifts to me

Do you seem to have little of Jesus' Spirit? Perhaps it is because you are not sharing what you do have of Him with others. Begin to serve, and you will begin to see Him serving through you. The blessing you give will be the blessing you receive in even greater measure. Only when you've emptied yourself can you be filled.

It is more blessed to give than to receive. ACTS 20:35

DAY 147

⚙ A reflection on BEING DRAWN TO GOD
When I need to remember the message of the Cross

Our Savior is the apex of all that is. There is nothing higher, no one greater. In great condescension, He came down, clothed Himself in human flesh, and lived among us, only to be lifted up in as shameful a way as humans can conceive. But that lifting up—the most evil thing humanity could have done—was the very thing that God used to draw us to Himself. Never let yourself cease to be drawn to Him.

When I am lifted up from the earth, I will draw everyone to myself. JOHN 12:32

☼ A reflection on BECOMING LIKE JESUS
When I want to reflect Jesus' humility

When we think of having the mind of Christ, we usually think in terms of getting His direction and following His will. We're focused on action. But God has a higher purpose. He is focused on character. When He gives us the mind of Jesus, He is giving us the one gift that will fundamentally alter our sinful, conflict-prone nature and shape us into the very image of God.

What is Jesus' mind like? In Philippians 2, Paul tells us of Jesus' humility. Though He was God incarnate, He was a humble, obedient servant—a dying servant, in fact. Humility isn't usually our goal when we strive for godly thinking, but it's the first element of character that God will work in us. If we haven't learned the humility of Jesus, we'll never really understand His resurrection power. Our prayers will lack strength because they lack the nature of a servant. Our work will lack power because it doesn't conform to His character. And our fellowship will lack unity because, unlike Jesus, we aren't looking out for each other's interests.

You must have the same attitude that Christ Jesus had.
PHILIPPIANS 2:5

☀ A reflection on BECOMING LIKE JESUS
When I need to think of others before myself

Human beings rarely aspire to become nothing. We want to make a name for ourselves, or at least to succeed at our goals. But the mind of Jesus will take us in the opposite direction. He found satisfaction in deferring to others' needs. He didn't cling to deity because, in the long run, a demonstration of power would be less satisfying than a demonstration of character. The godly agenda aims for wholeness and unity over authority and comfort. The divine program for exaltation and glory is to go through humility and meekness to get there.

If our minds are ever to be transformed into the likeness of Jesus, we have to learn to think that way. We must embrace deference, holding the welfare of others to be more valuable than our own. We must embrace service, working for the benefit of each other rather than trying to get ahead ourselves. And we must humble ourselves under the mighty hand of God in order for that hand to lift us up.

He gave up his divine privileges; he took the humble position of a slave and was born as a human being.
PHILIPPIANS 2:7

☼ A reflection on BECOMING LIKE JESUS
When I need to follow Jesus' example of obedience

Being like Jesus means more than healing and helping, preaching and teaching, feeding and clothing, and blessing at every turn. It also means obedience—deep, sacrificial, heartfelt obedience. The kind of obedience that requires ultimate humility, compelling us to subdue every dream that doesn't fit God's purposes. After all, the mind of Jesus led Him not to glory first, but to death.

God will not take us down easy paths to conform us to Jesus. He does not lead us on a walk in the park, but toward a struggle in the garden of Gethsemane, where strong wills are surrendered, and the glory of God and the welfare of others compete with our own personal plans. And we know, when we get there, that He will lead us into death.

It's a painful death, but a glorious one. The other side of it is resurrection, which God has planned all along. Our ultimate, humble obedience will lead to high exaltation. Why? Because a lowly-then-exalted Jesus has called us. The very mind of the Resurrection has become our guide.

When he appeared in human form, he humbled himself in obedience to God and died a criminal's death on a cross.
PHILIPPIANS 2:7-8

☼ A reflection on WAITING
When I need to be patient for God to act

It's against our nature to wait patiently when we think we might be able to affect an outcome. But the truth is, we often need to wait. We are to come to every situation with faith, an expectation of God's goodness, and a desire to do His will. While we would like these heart attitudes to be instantaneous, they rarely are. Therefore, we must approach each situation with time and thoughtfulness.

Whenever we find ourselves in a difficulty, instead of barging our way out of it along the path of least resistance, as we are prone to do, we must first ask the Lord His will, wait for His answer, and let Him take the initiative by preparing the way before us. His is not an instant way.

Ask yourself why it is sometimes hard to wait. Is it impatience with the situation? A desire to be in control? A suspicion that God is not going to intervene? Let God search your motives, and then search His will. Wait quietly until He reveals it in His timing. Waiting quietly demonstrates trust like nothing else. It is a way to honor Him.

It is good to wait quietly for salvation from the LORD.
LAMENTATIONS 3:26

☼ A reflection on LEGALISM
When I remember that Jesus is my righteousness

Centuries of legalism have given us an unfortunate interpretation of "the straight and narrow." Heaven, we are led to believe, is only for those who can live up to the demands of the gospel, and there are precious few who can.

However, the small gate and narrow road of which Jesus speaks is Himself. And the *only* people who find Him are those who give up walking the road themselves. When we make ourselves the gate—and we do, whenever we think our efforts are the key—we miss the true gate. "I tell you the truth, I am the gate for the sheep," Jesus says (John 10:7).

We lapse into self-effort frequently. Once saved by grace through faith in Him, we try to live by effort through faith in ourselves. We aim to be righteous, rather than trusting Him as our righteousness. But the narrow road *always* leads away from ourselves. *Everything* in the gospel is about Him. It's never our burden, and it's always full of grace.

The gateway to life is very narrow and the road is difficult, and only a few ever find it. MATTHEW 7:14

☯ A reflection on GOD'S GENEROSITY
When I need to be reminded that God gives abundantly

Many of us live under the impression that receiving gifts from God is like pulling teeth. We pray and plead for this or that blessing, often ignoring the precious gifts He has already given. But God is a giver. He has already given to us abundantly. He will continue to give. It is the Father's nature.

If you sinful people know how to give good gifts to your children, how much more will your heavenly Father give the Holy Spirit to those who ask him. LUKE 11:13

DAY 154

☯ A reflection on FAITHFULNESS
When I wonder if my service has any impact

We serve in a Kingdom of wheat kernels, mustard seeds, and hidden pearls—small things with huge impact. The world cannot see their value. In our more discouraging moments, neither can we. But do not be discouraged if your faithful service to God has imperceptible results. They are imperceptible only to the naked eye. They are highly valued in the eternal Kingdom, where those who give away their lives find them again.

I tell you the truth, unless a kernel of wheat is planted in the soil and dies, it remains alone. But its death will produce many new kernels—a plentiful harvest of new lives.
JOHN 12:24

☀ A reflection on WORSHIP
When I want to show true devotion to God

The greatest pleasure of the Christian life is worship. We approach it at first as an obligation. We're fairly self-focused, and it's hard to turn our hearts toward God. But if we do, in spirit and in truth (i.e., with zealous inspiration and according to who God really is), we find inexpressible delights.

Jesus would have us ask not which requirements we are to fulfill, but what more of ourselves we can offer Him. When we look for our required obligation, we do not worship in spirit, because the Spirit of God would not inspire us to fulfill quotas of devotion. And we do not worship in truth, because we underestimate God's worth. He is worth all we can give, and more.

Blessed is the worshiper who can truthfully—and with pleasure—say to the Lord: "What can I do for You? You name it, it's Yours. Whatever I can offer You, please let me." This is the kind of worshiper the Father seeks.

The time is coming—indeed it's here now—when true worshipers will worship the Father in spirit and in truth. The Father is looking for those who will worship him that way. JOHN 4:23

☼ A reflection on THE IMPOSSIBLE
When there seems to be no answer to my problems

We often limit our vision to what we know to be within the realm of possibility—not as God defines possibility, but as we define it. We forget the truth and need to hear it again: all things are possible with God.

Our Bible is full of impossible situations: A nation camped at the edge of a sea with a hostile army behind them. An inexperienced band of fighters faced an impenetrable, walled city. A shepherd boy stood before an armed and angry giant. A worshiper faced a lions' den. "Dry bones" rotted in a valley. And our only hope of salvation lay in a sealed tomb.

Have you reached a dead end? God does not promise to grant us everything on our agenda, but He does promise to meet real needs and to support real ministry in response to real faith. His track record is impressive. Never have His purposes been thwarted by circumstances too demanding. Never has His strength fallen short of the need. This is the promise we have in our Savior: all things are possible with God.

Jesus looked at them and said, "With man this is impossible, but not with God; all things are possible with God."
MARK 10:27, NIV

☀ A reflection on LISTENING TO GOD
When I need to let God's Word change my life

Recent surveys and demographic studies have indicated that Christians and non-Christians in the United States have remarkably similar behavior patterns. Why? Because many of us Christians stop at hearing and believing. We are not careful about how we listen. We are like those of whom James speaks: "For if you listen to the word and don't obey, it is like glancing at your face in a mirror. You see yourself, walk away, and forget what you look like" (James 1:23-24). This is a type of self-deceit. We think we are growing in the Word, but in reality we are growing in knowledge only. Real growth comes from real application—diligence in integrating the Word into our hearts and then living it. Careful listening brings radical change and lasting fruit.

God's purpose for His Word is that it be unhindered by testing, worries, riches, and pleasures. It is to be a seed that lands on our fertile soil, takes deep root, and grows steadily. Be careful. Listen in a way that will fulfill His purpose.

Pay attention to how you hear. To those who listen to my teaching, more understanding will be given. LUKE 8:18

☼ A reflection on TRUSTING GOD
When my faith is put to the test

How do you react in a crisis? Or, to ask an even more revealing question, how do you react in the minor irritations of everyday life? As much as we say that God is trustworthy and true, our tower of strength and our shield, those are only words until they are tested. And in this world, they are tested often. The truth of our relationship with God comes out when the heat is on. We discover whether we really trust Him only when we're put in a position of having to trust Him. A belief in God's providence means little until one lacks essentials, and a belief in God's strength means little until one is completely helpless. Then the truth comes out.

Where do you stand? Do you have a shallow belief in God's faithfulness, applying His promises to others' situations but not to your own? We must *know* who our Fortress is. We are not to become strong; we are to find our strength in Him. We must let His peace speak louder to us than our trials do. God stands firm when everything else moves. Can you?

The wicked are crushed by disaster, but the godly have a refuge when they die. PROVERBS 14:32

☼ A reflection on OBEDIENCE
When I want to show my love for Jesus

We have become so paranoid of having a theology of "righteousness = works" that we have ignored obedience altogether, as though it did not matter to God. Jesus is clear that it does. Obedience is not our means to righteousness; it is the clearest expression of our devotion to Jesus. It is meaningful worship. When we are disobedient, we are saying that God's Word does not matter to us. That isn't love.

As Christians, we need to recover a desire for obedience as an expression of love for our Savior. If we truly love Him, as we say we do, what He says will matter to us profoundly. We will not follow the acceptable parts of His teachings and ignore the objectionable parts. We will not approach our relationship with Him as though we are trying to get by with the bare minimum behavioral change. We will devour His teachings, turning them over in our hearts, meditating on their applications, and living them as clearly as we can. This, according to Jesus, is what loving Him is all about. This is genuine worship.

If you love me, obey my commandments. JOHN 14:15

⚙ A reflection on DISCIPLESHIP
When I want to focus on the Kingdom to come

Discipleship isn't about making a home in this world, it's about preparing for another. Discipleship is all about investing in the Kingdom of God rather than in the kingdom of this world. Anytime we face a choice between settling into this life and striving for a Kingdom still in formation, we must choose the latter. We simply cannot settle here; we're on a journey.

Jesus replied, "Foxes have dens to live in, and birds have nests, but the Son of Man has no place even to lay his head."
LUKE 9:58

DAY 161

⚙ A reflection on PERSISTENCE
When I need to keep seeking God

How many prayers have you dropped because God seemed not to be hearing? If He did not give a definite "no," He may have wanted the delay to draw you closer to Him and establish a better sense of His provision in your need. Don't just ask, seek, and knock; keep on asking, seeking, and knocking. Such times of persistence lead to a greater, more memorable experience of His goodness.

Everyone who asks, receives. Everyone who seeks, finds. And to everyone who knocks, the door will be opened.
MATTHEW 7:8

☼ A reflection on GRACE
When I am tempted to view God's favor cheaply

The apostle Paul asked this question: If all of our sins, present and future, are covered by the sacrifice of Jesus, should we keep on sinning? If none of this gospel is based on merit, should we just give up trying to behave ourselves? The answer to this question, according to Paul, is a horrified "Of course not!" Paul is clear on one thing we frequently forget: we did not simply sign a contract for our salvation; we exchanged lives with a Redeemer. He took our sinful selves into the grave with Him and brought us a resurrected life instead. And that life can never be comfortable with sin. Never.

If you view your salvation as a life-exchange rather than as a contractual agreement, then the very thought of sin will seem ludicrous. Yes, there will still be struggles, but not from any attempt to justify disobedience. The struggle will be only with the power of the flesh, which Jesus is ready and willing to subdue. With that kind of Savior, is there any reason at all to go on sinning?

Should we keep on sinning so that God can show us more and more of his wonderful grace? Of course not!
ROMANS 6:1-2

☼ A reflection on REFUGE
When I need to run to God, the source of my help

Why are so many of the Psalms about help and deliverance? Why is it so important to know God as our refuge? Because this is our greatest need. We might not think so. We think we need more fruit of the Spirit or more character; more possessions or power; more wisdom or talent. But God's assessment in the Bible is that we are sheep in need of a Shepherd, the oppressed in need of a Deliverer, the lost in need of a Savior. The other needs are important, too, but our first and foremost deficiency is our helplessness. It simply is not within us to be able to help ourselves.

Whatever our need is, it is met by looking away from ourselves and casting ourselves with abandon on our Savior. We must run to Him. He is the source of everything we need. He is the solution. In *everything* we are completely dependent on God. Need provision? It comes from Him. Protection? Also Him. Holiness? Again, from Him. You name the need, He is the source of supply. Learn to run to your Refuge.

O LORD my God, I take refuge in you. PSALM 7:1, NIV

☀ **A reflection on DOING WHAT IS RIGHT**
   When I wonder why my choices matter

In our individualistic culture, we tend to think that our behavior is our own domain. We hear and say things such as "It's my life," "It's my body," or "It's nobody's business but my own." Anyone claiming an absolute standard of behavior is sure to hear the mantra of the age: "As long as it's not hurting anyone else, it doesn't matter what a person does." God has a direct response: it matters. Why? Because those who are upright in heart and behavior show a respect for God and His ways. Those who are not—who are devious in their plans and destructive in their ways—show that they couldn't care less that God exists. What we think and what we do says a lot about the One we serve.

Have you made that connection between your lifestyle and your opinion of God? The two are intimately linked. Those who fear God with respect and awe will reflect it in their lives. Consider your thoughts, your words, and your actions well. Understand the statement you are making.

Those who follow the right path fear the LORD; those who take the wrong path despise him. PROVERBS 14:2

☼ A reflection on LOVING GOD
When I want my actions to show my devotion to Him

Many Christians get caught in an inconsistency between their words and their lives. It's quite common. We say we love God, but we fail repeatedly in our obedience, usually in one or two areas in particular. We have secret sins, nagging habits, and persistent character flaws that we just do not want to let go of. We know this, and we know God's desire for us to leave those things behind. But we don't; it's too hard. That's when we need to ask ourselves a deep question: "Do I really love Him?" That's the issue, isn't it? If we loved Him more than that habit, sin, or character flaw, we would have victory. We pursue the things we love most. If we hang on to our hidden faults, don't we love them more?

Jesus often used "love" and "obey" in the same sentence. It isn't a coincidence. It's a challenge. Search your soul. Decide whom you love, and obey Him with all your heart.

Those who accept my commandments and obey them are the ones who love me. JOHN 14:21

✺ A reflection on DISCIPLINE
When I need to see the Lord's love in His correction

We give no correction to strangers. Why? It's not our place
to do so; there's no relationship there. We can take comfort, then, in the fact that God disciplines us. It implies
that He loves us as children and is intent on our becoming
more like Him. He does not discipline those He has given
up on. He disciplines those He treasures.

Are you going through a hard thing today? It may be
discipline from the Lord to urge you to change something
in your life, or to help you develop greater endurance and
character. Regardless of its specific cause, it is designed to
shape you into His image, and it is monitored with great
care—even delight—by the hand from which it comes.
You would not be going through it if He did not care.
You would not be in the painful process of conforming
to His likeness if you were not His child. Cooperate with
His work, no matter how uncomfortable His tools are. He
does not use them recklessly. He uses them as lovingly as a
father touches his child.

*The LORD corrects those he loves, just as a father corrects
a child in whom he delights.* PROVERBS 3:12

☼ A reflection on LORDSHIP
When I need to evaluate Jesus' place in my life

Have you set limits on Jesus' authority in your affairs?
If you have determined aspects of your future by saying,
"I would never do that," or "I would never go there," then
you have placed limits on God. Expect Him to test them.
He will always try to stretch you out of your assumption
that you are in control of your life. Don't just call Him
"Lord." Make sure you do what He says.

*Why do you keep calling me "Lord, Lord!" when you don't
do what I say?* LUKE 6:46

DAY 168

☼ A reflection on SATISFACTION
When I hunger and thirst for righteousness

Where are your hunger and thirst directed? If you know
your own inadequacy and starve for a fulfillment that
comes from outside of yourself, then let your hunger
and thirst point you to the Bread of Life and the River of
Living Water. We hesitate to get our hopes up. We wonder
if our deep-down hunger for purity can ever be satisfied.
But Jesus never fails on a promise. We can be fulfilled. Let
your hopes—and your hunger—run wild.

*Blessed are those who hunger and thirst for righteousness,
for they will be filled.* MATTHEW 5:6, NIV

☼ A reflection on ETERNAL PERSPECTIVE
When I need to invest in what lasts forever

Human nature wants it all. We want to live forever in God's Presence, but we're reluctant to sacrifice anything in the meantime. We want heaven on earth as well as heaven in heaven. The fact that this is a spiritual impossibility doesn't faze us. We want it anyway.

Jesus doesn't offer His disciples an impossibility. He speaks in harsh realities. We must make a choice: invest ourselves in this life—which is passing and subject to decay—or invest in the Kingdom of God—which is eternal. There is no "all of the above" in Jesus' gospel presentation. It's either one or the other.

Can you honestly say that you care nothing for your life in this world? Or at least that your here-and-now plans pale in comparison to your hope in eternal life? If not, Jesus calls you to radically change your perspective. You cannot hang on to your visible life and your eternal life at the same time. One must be forsaken. Which will it be?

Those who love their life in this world will lose it. Those who care nothing for their life in this world will keep it for eternity.
JOHN 12:25

☼ **A reflection on UNBELIEF**
   When I feel myself resisting God

We tend to think of unbelief as the result of intellectual stumbling blocks to the gospel, or philosophical objections, or a lack of evidence and authentic miracles. But these things are usually cited by unbelievers simply as a covering for deeper issues. The real issue of unbelief is the inclination of the human heart. It wants to remain enthroned. It *cannot* accept a savior without denying its own ability to save.

Watch for this tendency in your own heart. Often we assent to Jesus mentally but resist Him deep within. Have you known this struggle? It's subtle, but human nature often is. We come across as enthusiastic believers, but the unbelief deep inside wants to put up a good fight. It wants to retain the right to a little bit of sin, to maintain a little autonomy. We often really want only a partial submission to our Creator. Let the Holy Spirit search—and transform—the deep places of your heart. Let Jesus complete His miracle in you.

Let us hold tightly without wavering to the hope we affirm.
HEBREWS 10:23

☀ A reflection on INTEGRITY
When I want God's truth to reach my heart

Psalm 51—King David's confessional psalm—contains an acknowledgment of one of God's greatest desires for us: integrity. God wants His truth and wisdom to reach to our core, not just adorn our outward expressions. He has no tolerance for hypocrisy. To the degree that His wisdom does not reach to our innermost parts—that His Spirit does not transform the very core of our being—then to that degree we have become like the scribes of Jesus' day: experts in the Word but devoid of its power. Our mouths speak godliness, but our hearts deny it. None of us is perfect in our integrity, of course. We all have inconsistencies. But those inconsistencies should be steadily disappearing if we are growing in the strength of God's Spirit.

Test yourself often. Do the words of your mouth reflect the thoughts of your heart? Like David, we must know that God is zealous for our consistency. We must reflect Him from within, or we don't reflect Him at all.

Surely you desire truth in the inner parts; you teach me wisdom in the inmost place. PSALM 51:6, NIV

☼ A reflection on BECOMING LIKE CHRIST
When I want to be more like Jesus

One of the ways we can determine whether we are becoming Christlike is to see how we act in a crisis. When the pressure is on, what motives will direct us? Jesus was clear about His purpose in coming to Jerusalem; He would die there. And now the time had come. Jesus did not ask God to save Him from this hour (see John 12:27), but when He got to the garden of Gethsemane, He wanted to know if it would be possible for the cup of suffering to pass Him by (Matthew 26; Mark 14; Luke 22). In the middle of His crisis, though, one motive still guided Him: He preferred the glory of God's name over His own self-preservation. God's reputation weighed heavier on His heart than His own comfort and life.

It is God's plan for you to be conformed to the image of His Son. Examine your motives, especially in the midst of a crisis. Do you prefer the glory of God to your own escape? Imitate Christ. Let your actions glorify God.

[Jesus said,] "Should I pray, 'Father, save me from this hour'? But this is the very reason I came! Father, bring glory to your name." JOHN 12:27-28

☀ A reflection on LOVING OTHERS
When I am struggling to love my enemies

God commands us to love others. And He specifically commands us to love those who actively seek to do us harm. There is absolutely nothing in it for us, at least on the surface. And yet it is not just a suggestion; it is a command. There is no one on the planet from whom we are told to withhold love.

Think about those whom you can consider enemies, or who have declared themselves your opponents. Perhaps they disagree with your faith or your politics; perhaps they have betrayed your confidence; perhaps it's just a personality conflict. Make a list. Then review the list with an understanding that everyone on it is to be the object of your love. Is this possible? Humanly speaking, no. We can no more manufacture love than we could save ourselves from sin. Ask God, the author of all love, to love them through you.

[Jesus said,] "You have heard the law that says, 'Love your neighbor' and hate your enemy. But I say, love your enemies! Pray for those who persecute you!" MATTHEW 5:43-44

✸ A reflection on PERSECUTION
When I need to rejoice in suffering

Jesus' words—telling us that we're blessed when others hate us because of our faith—prepare us for any trial by pointing us to eternal realities. Is God's Kingdom where we've placed our hopes? If so, we will not only tolerate our rejection by this world, but we'll see it as happy confirmation that we are in union with Jesus.

What blessings await you when people hate you . . . because you follow the Son of Man. When that happens, be happy! Yes, leap for joy! For a great reward awaits you in heaven.
LUKE 6:22-23

DAY 175

✸ A reflection on FAILURE
When I am thinking about the times my faith has wavered

We tend to dwell on our faltering efforts at faith, remembering well the falls we've taken along the way to maturity. We should not take them lightly, but neither should we let them define us. Jesus saw Simon Peter's denial in advance, yet He prayed with confidence that his faith would not fail. In the final analysis, it did not. And that's what counts with Jesus. Do not let your failures define you. Trust Jesus. He has prayed for you.

I have pleaded in prayer for you, Simon, that your faith should not fail. LUKE 22:32

☀ A reflection on THE CHARACTER OF GOD
When I need a reminder of who God is

Occasionally in the Old Testament, God is referred to as Father, but He is never addressed in prayer as Father. Jesus' intimate opening to what we now call the Lord's Prayer—"Our Father in heaven"—may have stunned His listeners. That level of familiarity made God out to be accessible and affectionate—not easy concepts for those of us steeped in formal religion.

As soon as Jesus tells us of the intimacy with God that is available to us, He stresses the utter transcendence and "otherness" of God—His holiness. "Hallowed be your name," He says (NIV). In two brief phrases, He has captured the essence of our relationship with God. It is at once intimate and unfathomable; familiar yet mysterious. Though we may know Him deeply, we will never know Him fully.

We often take this opening to the Lord's Prayer to be a prelude, similar to the salutation of a letter. But this particular salutation is actually the substance of our faith. It captures both the closeness of God and His unreachable distance. Meditate on its riches. The greatest commandment—to love our transcendent Father with all of our being—begins here.

Our Father in heaven, may your name be kept holy.
MATTHEW 6:9

☼ A reflection on GENEROSITY
When I need to follow the call to radical giving

God's call to a radical change of lifestyle includes a radical change of our emotional investment in our money and our things. We are to use the currency of this world—materials and money—to strengthen the currency of the Kingdom—faith. This often means that we will have to give away our holdings to those who ask for them or who need them and are afraid to ask. We must hold everything with a loose grip.

"I have little to give," we might complain. But this excuse does not hold up. If we have little, we must give little. Jesus commended the woman who dropped only two small coins into the coffer. Why did she give all she had? Because it was all she could give.

Jesus calls us to be radical. Sacrificially radical and sacrificially generous.

If you lend money only to those who can repay you, why should you get credit? Even sinners will lend to other sinners for a full return. LUKE 6:34

❀ A reflection on WHAT WILL LAST

*When I am ready to spend my life on things
that matter*

Other than God Himself, only two things are mentioned in Scripture as lasting forever: the Word of God and the souls of human beings. These two areas are where Jesus calls us to involve ourselves. No genuine investment in them will spoil; they are the "food that endures."

As Christians, we need to inventory our lives. How do we spend our time? How do we spend our money? Where is our energy going? What do we think about when we lie down at night and when we wake up in the morning? When the world itself passes away, what of our work will remain? Answering these questions regularly will keep our lives on track and give us focus.

Jesus gives us very clear instructions in approaching these questions. "Do not work for food that spoils," He tells us. Our lives should be entirely eternity-focused. We were created to bear fruit that lasts (John 15:16). When we invest ourselves in anything else, we are falling short of our purpose, missing the abiding joy of Kingdom fruitfulness. Work for food that endures.

*Do not work for food that spoils, but for food that endures
to eternal life, which the Son of Man will give you.*
JOHN 6:27, NIV

☀ A reflection on JOY
When I want to experience deep satisfaction

Jesus' intent is for every Christian to have joy. Why then do so many of us struggle to have it?

When Jesus speaks to His disciples about joy in John 15, He has just told them to remain in His love—through obedience (verses 9-10). And He goes on to tell them to love each other as He has loved them (verse 12). It isn't a suggestion; it's a command. The result will be joyful lives. It isn't a difficult formula in principle—just in practice. When we do not have joy in our lives, it is because we have left something out of the formula. We have not remembered the wealth of Jesus' love, or we have not loved others as extravagantly as He has loved us.

It seems as if it should be more difficult than this. We think that to have joy, something must happen to change our circumstances or heal our past wounds. All the while, Jesus asks us to look past the surface of our joylessness and major on love.

I have told you these things so that you will be filled with my joy. Yes, your joy will overflow! JOHN 15:11

⚙ A reflection on VICTORY
When I am reminded that God's Kingdom will
ultimately prevail

Few of us knew that the day we became a Christian was
the day we enlisted in the armed forces. To be a citizen
of the Kingdom of God is to be a soldier in its military.
And victory belongs to those whose hearts are completely
God's. We may wonder, in this fallen world, why it often
seems to elude us; but the problem is likely in our definition of victory. Yes, we will be wounded at times, and
eventually death comes to all. But for the faithful, these
things never come at the wrong time, and never without
a promise. God's Kingdom purposes will be established
through us. Victory is certain.

A wise assessment of our struggles will always include
this glorious fact: almighty God fights on behalf of those
whose hearts are His. When we look at a problem with
a sense of defeat, we are not wise to the reality of God's
power or His promise. We must always know who holds
victory in His hand, and we must never lose heart.

Thank God! He gives us victory over sin and death through
our Lord Jesus Christ. 1 CORINTHIANS 15:57

❋ A reflection on GOD'S PURPOSES
When I need to remember that God is sovereign

When your situation is critical, remember the calm of Jesus in the midst of His greatest storm—speaking to Pilate before His crucifixion. He acknowledged God's sovereignty over His circumstances. Remember, too, the principle Paul lays down for us: "In *all things* God works for the good of those who love him, who have been called according to his purpose" (Romans 8:28, NIV, italics added). Are you in a difficult place? God is accomplishing His purpose through it.

Jesus said [to Pilate], "You would have no power over me at all unless it were given to you from above." JOHN 19:11

DAY 182

❋ A reflection on REST
When I am working so hard to please God

Too often we get caught up in the folly of self-effort. We think our provision is up to us, so we struggle. We think our righteousness is up to us, so we strain. We think our spirituality is a work of human willpower, so we press on even harder. All the while, Jesus says to us: "Come to *Me*." He will give us rest. Faith and complete dependence on Jesus are to precede obedience. Take His yoke and let Him lead.

Come to me, all of you who are weary and carry heavy burdens, and I will give you rest. MATTHEW 11:28

DAY 183

☀ A reflection on FEAR
When I am overcome with anxiety

Storms swell, sometimes gradually on the horizon, and sometimes suddenly and furiously, without warning. Either way, fear is usually our first reaction. It isn't that we overestimate the storms; we've seen them destroy the lives of other people, so we know they can be damaging. No, our problem is in having an inaccurate view of Jesus. As long as we're preoccupied with the storm, we will fear. It is a natural—and inevitable—human response.

But Jesus asks us to do the unnatural and avoid the inevitabilities of our human frailties. He asks us to have faith in Him. Yes, the storm is dangerous. Yes, we are weak and vulnerable. Left with those two facts alone, we are overcome. But Jesus gives us another fact to throw into the equation—Himself. He is the King of all creation, God with us. With our eyes fixed on Him, we can say, "What storm? What danger? What weakness?" The storms *must* obey Him. What do we have to fear?

God is our refuge and strength, always ready to help in times of trouble. So we will not fear when earthquakes come and the mountains crumble into the sea. PSALM 46:1-2

DAY 184

⚙ **A reflection on FINDING TRUE LIFE**
When I need to refocus on the life of the Spirit

God's Kingdom is so encompassing, so eternal, so all-consuming that it means everything. It is life—the source of life, the abundance of life, the destiny of life. This world that we see with our eyes and spend most of our lives obsessing about means nothing as an end in itself. It exists as a very good part of God's creation, but it has no value apart from life in the Spirit.

Disciples of Jesus must take on His spiritual nature. We must live with eternal perspectives, considering ourselves citizens of a spiritual Kingdom. We must understand that the Spirit gives life and that this world counts for nothing.

Jesus tells us to partake of Him. His is the life that we must take upon ourselves; His words gives us life through His Spirit. We must daily reorient ourselves from the life of the flesh to the life of the Spirit. All of our decisions must be spiritually appraised from an eternal, Kingdom-conscious perspective. Life can be found nowhere else.

The Spirit alone gives eternal life. Human effort accomplishes nothing. And the very words I have spoken to you are spirit and life. JOHN 6:63

☼ A reflection on GOD'S PROTECTION
When I am overwhelmed and losing hope

Are you bogged down in the burdens of life? Are you overwhelmed by the spiritual battles you are in? Are you losing hope? Do not forget this principle: what you see is not all there is. The "visible" and the "real" are two vastly different things, and the invisible God is more real than the visible enemy. Tens of thousands are hopelessly powerless in the face of His power. Above and beyond your problems are: (1) the power of the Lord of hosts; (2) all of His obedient servants ready to do warfare on your behalf; and (3) your prayers and your faith—the clear lines of communication between you and your Deliverer.

Like David in Psalm 3, we can refuse to be intimidated by the tens of thousands drawn up against us. Why? Because we know a Savior infinitely stronger than tens of thousands. This is not an irrational hope. It is not escapism. It is reality. We have no reason to fear.

I lay down and slept, yet I woke up in safety, for the LORD was watching over me. I am not afraid of ten thousand enemies who surround me on every side. PSALM 3:5-6

☼ **A reflection on CHANGE**
When I need to be ready to leave old ways behind

Jesus approaches a man who has been an invalid for thirty-eight years. The Son of God, with all of His insight into peoples' hearts, comes to him with what seems like a no-brainer of a question. "Would you like to get well?"

Jesus knows that sometimes, as much as we think we want change, we're comfortable with the status quo. We say we want to be delivered of our sins, but we still look for ways to be tempted by them. We ask to be filled with His Spirit, but we're scared to death of what He'll have us do. We want to change, but we don't want to change. We're divided souls.

Jesus comes to us with the same pointed question: "Would you like to get well?" We must be prepared for radical change if we want a real encounter with Him. We must be willing to leave old ways behind. If we really want to know Him, we must first know that nothing will ever be the same again.

When Jesus saw him and knew he had been ill for a long time, he asked him, "Would you like to get well?"
JOHN 5:6

☼ A reflection on LISTENING TO GOD
When I need to be open to Jesus' teachings

Jesus uses the statement "Anyone with ears to hear should listen and understand" multiple times in the Gospels and Revelation. It's clear that Jesus knows that some will be ready to receive His message enthusiastically. And with that clear expectation comes the negative implication: some will not. There are stubborn hearts in this world, people "without ears," those who will not open themselves to the possibility of the truth of the gospel.

Rebellious souls cannot hear the words of Jesus—really hear them—until they recognize and acknowledge their own insufficiency. Even as believers, we must always be aware of our need for God. We need to be on guard against our natural gravitation toward rebellion and its inevitable result—deafness.

Jesus almost always uses this phrase after a difficult message. His hard teachings are often a stumbling block, but we can use them as a true test of the openness of our hearts. When Jesus' words grate against our natural inclinations, we must ask ourselves, "Do I have ears to hear?" How we respond will indicate the condition of our hearts.

Anyone with ears to hear should listen and understand.
LUKE 8:8

⚘ A reflection on DESPAIR
When I am overcome with spiritual struggles

We face intense struggles in our Christian life. Circumstances rise up against us; our devotion to God is threatened by temptation; and persecution is inevitable for those who stand faithful in Christ. Looking at our natural capabilities, we will despair at the supernatural battle that comes against us. But despair leads us to Jesus. The answer cannot come from ourselves—we are too weak. When Jesus says, "To him who overcomes," He is telling us to rest faithfully in Him.

To him who overcomes, I will give the right to eat from the tree of life. REVELATION 2:7, NIV

DAY 189

⚘ A reflection on SECURITY
When I am afraid for my physical safety

Where does your security lie? Real safety is found in standing firm with God. He is our protector and defender. Even when we walk through the valley of the shadow of death, we need not fear any evil; the Good Shepherd is with us. Our safety is contingent only on our faith in Him (Luke 12:4-5). Let God redefine your understanding of security.

Even when I walk through the darkest valley, I will not be afraid, for you are close beside me. PSALM 23:4

☀ A reflection on TRUSTING GOD
When I need to have faith in God's wisdom for my life

The best advice we can find in Proverbs repeatedly points us to a wisdom beyond our own. God is worthy of all of our trust. We are not dependable; our knowledge is limited and our motives are not pure. Yet we often struggle to decide whether to lean on His wisdom or our own. His can seem so hard, but we forget that ours is harder. After all, there are ominous consequences for depending on our own limited resources.

Trust is not natural to the fallen human heart. The redeemed heart has to learn it. We must make a conscious decision to forsake our own understanding and lean on His. When crises confront you, use them as opportunities to drink in the wisdom of the Source of all wisdom.

Are you faced with a choice today? Make up your mind not to act on it until you have sought God's wisdom diligently, persistently, and patiently. Ask Him for it. Follow it, no matter how hard it is. Let His mind become yours.

Trust in the LORD with all your heart; do not depend on your own understanding. PROVERBS 3:5

☼ A reflection on SINGLE-MINDEDNESS
When I need to fix my eyes only on Jesus

The request from Jesus' would-be follower in Luke 9 doesn't seem out of line. Everyone, when setting out on an adventure, says good-bye to his or her family. So why does Jesus have a problem with this request from a potential disciple?

Jesus does not want us looking back. The issue isn't a casual good-bye. The issue is where the heart is focused. Jesus' call is always immediate and thorough. The timing of His call is never an accident. When He calls, it is the appropriate time to turn our hearts solely toward Him.

What hinders your service in the Kingdom? Is anything constantly drawing your attention in another direction than Jesus? If so, it must be dealt with. We often let the preoccupations of life—relationships, careers, possessions, interests—distract our gaze. But we serve a God who is intent on winning our hearts. Jesus welcomes any disciple who is prepared to follow wholeheartedly. Let your eyes fall on Him alone.

Another said, "Yes, Lord, I will follow you, but first let me say good-bye to my family." But Jesus told him, "Anyone who puts a hand to the plow and then looks back is not fit for the Kingdom of God." LUKE 9:61-62

☼ A reflection on FEAR
When I am afraid

Life is full of circumstances that are terrifying at first glance and can consume us with worries about the future. Financial crises, health crises, spiritual dilemmas, and emotional needs cause us much stress. But here is the lesson learned by the disciples when Jesus walked to them on water: what initially made them panic was the very Person who brought them growth, faith, rest, and guidance.

Our crises can do the same. Though our initial reaction may be panic, in reality Jesus may be coming to us with a crisis that heals, strengthens, encourages, or guides. To us, our problems are threatening. To God, they are often the very means to develop us as His disciples. They may bear eternal fruit that our terrified eyes cannot at first see.

Will we, like the disciples, take Jesus "into the boat" (John 6:21, NIV)? When they did, John reports, they immediately reached the shore. Their panic—like ours most often is—had been unfounded. Jesus brings them, and us, safely to solid ground.

Suddenly [the disciples] saw Jesus walking on the water toward the boat. They were terrified, but he called out to them, "Don't be afraid. I am here!" JOHN 6:19-20

☼ **A reflection on MERCY**
When I want to know God more fully

Consider the mystery of a God who creates a race of people that He fully knows will collapse into rebellion, simply so He can redeem that race. Consider the oddity of a righteous and holy God who bypasses those who have tried on their own to clean themselves up in order to demonstrate grace to those who haven't. Who may know the mind of this God?

God desires to be known in His mercy. Not just mercy, in fact, but incomprehensibly *extravagant* mercy. Mindboggling mercy. The kind of mercy that bridges such a vast expanse that those who see it are compelled to fall on their faces in gratitude and worship. Do you know this mercy? We who realize we need a Savior must find our place with the tax collectors and sinners and drink it in. As we do, we'll be learning the mind of God.

When Jesus heard this, he told them, "Healthy people don't need a doctor—sick people do. I have come to call not those who think they are righteous, but those who know they are sinners." MARK 2:17

☀ A reflection on RESURRECTION
When I think of my true identity

God's people are called a lot of things in Scripture, including sinners, sheep without a shepherd, blind, lost, and idolatrous. But none of that matters when someone meets Christ. We are in a new category of creation. We are now "children of the resurrection" (Luke 20:36).

When we're kicking ourselves for past failures, we need only look at the resurrection of Jesus and know that we are new children. When all the world surrounds us with its pettiness, bitterness, and rage, we can live in a transcendent way, with our hope and all of our values fixed firmly above the mess. When we are sitting at the deathbed of a loved one, or even lying in our own, we can remember the empty grave and know that no child of the Resurrection is contained by it.

Children of the Resurrection can stand out for their vitality, their hope, their faith, their way of life and love. We are members of a new creation. Remember that when you encounter the old one.

They are children of God and children of the resurrection.
LUKE 20:36

☼ A reflection on GOD'S REALITY
When I need to base my faith on the power of God

Is your faith realistic? It shouldn't be—not by the world's standards, anyway. It should be completely in line with the will and the ways of God, but it should not conform to the world's expectations. Jesus ignores the ridicule of an unbelieving crowd, just as He did before He healed Jairus's daughter (see Mark 5:35-43). We should too. Faith knows things they don't know. God's reality is higher than human expectations—always. Raise your expectations to reflect His reality.

He went inside and asked, "Why all this commotion and weeping? The child isn't dead; she's only asleep."
MARK 5:39

DAY 196

☼ A reflection on GRACE
When I want to remember God's astonishing kindness

Whenever your faith grows apathetic, whenever your sense of His grace grows dim, whenever your mercy toward others finds its limits—contemplate the staggering absurdity of the infinitely Holy God suffering the consequences for those who rejected His holiness. Let His grace amaze you and prompt your zealous, passionate worship.

God made Christ, who never sinned, to be the offering for our sin, so that we could be made right with God through Christ. 2 CORINTHIANS 5:21

☼ A reflection on INTERCESSORY PRAYER
When I need to persevere on behalf of others

You may have wondered if your prayers are effective. We have all felt, at times, as though we were trying to persuade a reluctant God to intervene in a situation that He'd prefer to leave alone. Yet God has made prayer an integral part of His activity in this world. In fact, through Scripture He gives us the impression that His activity in the affairs of men is somehow contingent on the prayers of intercessors. If we don't pray, He doesn't act. It is His plan for us to ask; when we don't, we violate His plan.

Has the Holy Spirit prompted you to pray for someone? You *must* follow through on it! His prompting was not superfluous; He is efficient with His directions, and He would not have led you unless your prayers were an essential aspect of His intervention. We must continue in our prayer assignments until God's work is done. When His Spirit assures us that our prayers are complete, we may move on to others—but not before. His plan may hinge on your pleadings. Plead however—and whenever—He leads.

I will certainly not sin against the LORD by ending my prayers for you. I SAMUEL 12:23

☼ A reflection on LOVING GOD
When I want to increase my passion for God

Are you interested in praying a prayer that could revolutionize your life? Try this: begin each day by asking God a series of questions. "Lord, how can I love You today? What act of worship can I do? What words can I utter that will honor and bless You? What act of service can I do to represent Your love? How would Your Spirit inspire me to pray today?"

If you ask questions like this and watch for ways God might answer throughout your days, you'll find something happening deep within your soul. You'll find that worship becomes a lifestyle. You'll find that your faith becomes less centered on you and more centered on God. You'll find that the greatest commandment—to love God with all your heart, soul, strength, and mind—becomes your greatest desire. If you think your relationship with God is cold and passionless, you'll find it melting in the warmth of His favor. You'll experience His love in deeper ways than you ever have.

I have loved you even as the Father has loved me. Remain in my love. JOHN 15:9

☼ A reflection on FLEXIBILITY
When I need to be ready to respond to God

The God we serve is not unreasonable or inconsistent, but He *is* unpredictable. No human has ever fathomed His ways. Anyone who follows Him must quickly learn: He is not a formula. He does not repeat the same methods over and over again. He does not let us get into a habit of obedience-by-memory that does not engage the spirit. There is great mercy in that. He is a God of relationship, and He only allows us to relate to Him. We cannot memorize Him, we cannot learn His principles apart from His Person, and we cannot substitute His law in place of His Spirit. He desires to be known, and while His past deeds help us know who He is, His present direction can only be found in a vital relationship with His Person.

In your discipleship, are you depending on principles, or are you looking for God? You must be available to do what He commands today, not what He commanded you last time. Know the difference. Know your God.

If only you would listen to his voice today! PSALM 95:7

☼ A reflection on GOD'S PATIENCE
When I am thankful for a God who waits

We were once citizens of a distant country. God didn't exile us there; we moved there of our own accord. Like the Prodigal Son, we were happy to be independent, away from the stifling Presence of the Father, though hypocritically satisfied with His wealth. We celebrated and squandered, thinking we were accountable only to ourselves and forfeiting any right we may have ever had to call ourselves His children.

Many in our society still act as if independence were the highest virtue. Many are still living in a distant country. Meanwhile, our Father waits. He knows the futility of His children's independence; He knows it will bring them to ruin. But unless they see it themselves, they will not believe it. So He waits.

The waiting Father is a beautiful and welcome picture for those of us who may have wondered if our failures would cause the Father to turn His back on us. We know He is righteous, and we know we are not. We may think we are no longer welcome in His house. But Jesus' illustration is clear. We have a Father who waits.

He returned home to his father. And while he was still a long way off, his father saw him coming. LUKE 15:20

☀ **A reflection on GOD'S CHARACTER**
   When I am trying to hide from God

The Father whom Jesus portrays in the story of the Prodigal Son is a God who runs to meet His children. Never mind the child's past. His former rebellious arrogance is no longer an issue. Neither are the rags he's wearing when he returns. The Father enthusiastically runs to His child and escorts him into His household.

Jesus' portrayal of the Father is contrary to human nature and contrary to all our expectations. Like Adam and Eve in the Garden, we often hide from Him when we have sinned. We think he'll be angry, not glad to see us.

But our God runs to us. That's what the Incarnation and the Cross are all about. In spite of our rags, the lingering smell of the pigsty, the empty pockets, and the embarrassment that colors our faces, He throws His arms around us and kisses us. May we daily give thanks for such a Father. We can base our lives on the knowledge that we are irrevocably His.

While he was still a long way off, his father saw him coming. Filled with love and compassion, he ran to his son, embraced him, and kissed him. LUKE 15:20

☼ A reflection on PURSUING THE LOST
*When I need encouragement to share God's love
with others*

We may sometimes think that in our relationship with
God, we were the pursuers and He was the recluse. But
this is not so. Jesus is the pursuer incarnate. As in the story
of the Prodigal Son, the Father goes to the older brothers
of the world and pleads. We live in a world of many who
refuse to understand God. Still, the Father goes and pleads.
He sent His Son for this purpose. And His Son sends us.

*The older brother was angry and wouldn't go in. His father
came out and begged him.* LUKE 15:28

DAY 203

☼ A reflection on FREEDOM
When I need to be released from sinful habits

Are you comfortable with certain sinful aspects of your
life? Perhaps you once struggled in those areas but finally
gave up trying. And that's the problem. You gave up
because you found that you couldn't overcome your sin.
But it's the *Son* who overcomes; He sets us free. Abandon
mediocrity, rest in His strength, and *never* settle for anything less than complete purity. He calls you to be free
indeed.

If the Son sets you free, you are truly free. JOHN 8:36

☼ A reflection on LORDSHIP
When I need to remember that Jesus alone is Lord

The scandalous claim of Jesus is that He is the only way to God—the unique entrance into knowing who God is. The exclusiveness of Jesus' claims contradicts the spirit of our age. People want an adviser, not a Lord. They want a mentor, not a Master. It's simply too demanding to follow one Lord to the exclusion of all others.

Doesn't this mind-set seep into the Christian's perspective as well? Most of us know that we should reject such a compromising view of the Savior. But in practice, how many lords do we really have? Most of us could probably identify rivals to Jesus to whom we sometimes bow. A career field? A political perspective? A relationship? A lifestyle? A philosophy? We daily consume information from a variety of sources, many of which tell us another way, another truth, another life. We try to ignore them, but sometimes we accommodate them. We let many sources direct us, when in reality there is only one revelation— Jesus Himself. His claim is exclusive, and we hesitate to narrow ourselves to Him alone. But that's what He insists on. He's the only way.

I am the way, the truth, and the life. No one can come to the Father except through me. JOHN 14:6

☼ A reflection on SEEKING GOD
When I want God to be first in my thoughts

The call of God is all about seeking. Jesus constantly calls His disciples to set their hearts on Him, denying the supremacy of any other loves and declaring His alone. Most of us who believe in Jesus want our hearts to be directed rightly, but there are competing interests involved. Some of them are good; none of them are worth elevating higher than Jesus. But in the confusion of competing calls, how can we be sure His Kingdom is our first pursuit?

Try this diagnostic test: make a mental note of what occupies your thoughts. Your checkbook and your schedule may indicate your priorities well, but a better indication is what you think about. What fills your mind when you lie down to sleep at night? When you wake up in the morning? When you find yourself daydreaming in the middle of the day? If you detect a dominant pattern or a theme, know that this is where your heart lies.

Do this test and determine to make God preeminent in your affections. Be careful about what you seek first.

Seek the Kingdom of God above all else, and live righteously, and he will give you everything you need. MATTHEW 6:33

☼ A reflection on DISCIPLESHIP
When I want to know the Person of Jesus

One of the greatest temptations Christians face is to avert our eyes from the Person of Jesus and place them on the things of Jesus—His doctrine, His people, His Word, or His mission. These things are essential, but when we focus on them as objective entities apart from living fellowship with the Person of Jesus, they become hollow.

This is why Jesus doesn't call His disciples by saying "Follow My teachings," or "Follow My example," or "Follow My reasoning." It is always personal: "Follow Me." Too many believers have a sterile faith that emphasizes the impersonal aspects of Jesus. But He will not let us be content with that. He confronts us with Himself.

As good and instructive as theology and doctrine can be, we must not turn to them as the substance of our faith. Jesus is not a system of belief. Daily study and application are not enough. These must be built on daily communication—two-way communication between us and Jesus Himself. Wherever your discipleship is today, make sure it remains intensely personal.

"Follow me and be my disciple," Jesus said. MATTHEW 9:9

☼ A reflection on STRENGTH
When I want to live in Jesus' power

In Luke 9, we find Jesus commissioning His disciples for their first mission—to blanket the area with the Good News of His Kingdom. He gives them power and authority over demons and diseases, a considerable wealth to carry with them (verse 1). But He prohibits their carrying any materials. They are loaded with power but light as a feather. They can go in His strength and not in their own.

How are you living out your mission? Are you drawing your strength from Jesus' power and authority? Or are you depending on the props? Those who go through life carrying sacks of provisions find themselves powerless; they have unwittingly confessed a mistrust in God's providence. Those who go through life unencumbered find that His strength accompanies them in abundance.

What encumbers you? You will need to get rid of it, or at least change your attitude toward it. Know the difference between living in His power and on your self-reliance. Carry out your mission full of His strength and unburdened by your own.

"Take nothing for your journey," he instructed them. *"Don't take a walking stick, a traveler's bag, food, money, or even a change of clothes."* LUKE 9:3

⚙ A reflection on OFFERING
When I want to give myself to God

The story is a familiar one to many: In the days preceding Jesus' death, a woman breaks open a clay jar of expensive perfume and anoints Him with it. He says she has done a beautiful thing.

Like the vessel of nard, we believers are also to be broken and poured out at the feet of the Savior, as He was broken and emptied for us. We may be tempted at times to feel as if our service for the Lord is a waste of time and resources. Like Mary's act of service, ours may bear no visible fruit, and it may impress no one else at the party. But motivation is the key. Is it done in pure devotion? Is it an offering of the best we have for the One we treasure most? Is it prompted by a passion for the character and work of our Savior? Then it is not a waste. A vessel broken so that its treasure might be devoted to Jesus is the kind of sacrifice that pleases Him most. It is what He asks of us, and it is a fragrant aroma to Him. It is a beautiful thing.

She has done a beautiful thing to me. MARK 14:6, NIV

✺ A reflection on THE HEART OF GOD
When I want my life to reflect God's character

It's easy to be so outwardly focused that we're inwardly bankrupt. Do you ever go through the rituals of a worship service without an attitude of worship? Are you so focused on law that you condemn the lawless? God's character is the source of justice, mercy, faithfulness, love, compassion, and truth. Whatever we do in His name should be saturated with such attributes. If it isn't, then like the Pharisees, we've "swallowed a camel." We've missed the heart of God.

You strain your water so you won't accidentally swallow a gnat, but you swallow a camel! MATTHEW 23:24

DAY 210

✺ A reflection on JESUS' COMING
When I want to live in expectation of Jesus' return

Many Christians wonder not only when Jesus' second coming will be—which we cannot know—but also what it will look like. Some may wonder if, in fact, He has already come. Will we recognize Him? Jesus' prophecy is absolutely clear. His return will be glorious, everyone will know it, and no one will doubt whether it is the real event. Do not be deceived, and live each day in full anticipation of His sudden, visible return.

As the lightning flashes in the east and shines to the west, so it will be when the Son of Man comes. MATTHEW 24:27

☼ A reflection on EVANGELISM
When I am challenged to follow the great commission

Nearly two millennia after the ascension of Jesus, huge pockets of people still have *never* heard that there is a Savior from the awful devastation of sin and death. We are uncomfortable that thousands of children on other continents starve to death, but we are numb to the eternal hunger of billions. Isn't God more urgent than this? Is His passion to save really this sluggish?

The God who pursues has issued a directive. The disciples of the High Commander are ordered to pray for pursuers to rush into His harvest, and even to go. It's an urgent appeal, and it's comprehensive as well. Through the great commission, we are called to do more than spread the Word verbally; we are called to live it everywhere. Like light that floods a dark room, salt that influences a whole meal, or leaven that raises an entire loaf, we are urged to follow in the footsteps of the One who came to save.

Jesus' command is comprehensive, compelling, and urgent. Give. Pray. Go. Die, if necessary. Fill the world with His glory.

Go and make disciples of all the nations, baptizing them in the name of the Father and the Son and the Holy Spirit.
MATTHEW 28:19

☼ A reflection on GOD'S WORD
When I need to be reminded of the authority of Scripture

Jesus Himself says that He is the Alpha and Omega, the beginning and the end. When this truth grips us, discipleship takes off. There can be no casual reading of the Gospels when we understand that the words of Jesus are the words not only of a great teacher but of God Himself, the Creator of the universe, the author of all wisdom and the knower of all mysteries. There is nothing truer or more complete in this world than the teaching that comes straight from the mouth of the living God; in fact, there is no other opinion worth heeding. His words are the owner's manual for our hearts.

Ask yourself these probing questions: Do you hear His words casually, as though they are mere suggestions? Or do you voraciously consume His teaching as the key to life, dependent on it for your very existence? Are His words like a fragrant aroma—pleasing, but not entirely necessary? Or are they like oxygen—a matter of life and death? His words were true before the foundation of the world and they will be true for all eternity. Savor them well.

I am the Alpha and the Omega, the First and the Last, the Beginning and the End. REVELATION 22:13

☼ A reflection on THE GOOD SHEPHERD
When I need Jesus' protection

Anyone who has ever worked with sheep will attest to this fact: sheep are stupid. They wander off without any sense of direction; they often do not recognize danger when it is present, and even when they do recognize it, they do nothing in defense. Of all God's creatures, they are some of the most vulnerable and simple. And this is exactly the image Jesus uses for us.

Anyone who has ever been a shepherd will attest to this fact: it is servile, thankless labor that offers no rewards in the eyes of the world. And this is exactly the image Jesus uses for Himself.

The sheep's relationship to the shepherd is one of absolute dependence and protection. When a sheep wanders off and gets stuck in a ditch, the shepherd must find it, pull it out, and compel it to come back. If he does not, it will die in its predicament. But a good shepherd always does.

The sheep-shepherd relationship is a humble picture, but it is a comforting and compelling illustration of us and our Savior. Think about it the next time you're stuck in a ditch.

I am the good shepherd. The good shepherd sacrifices his life for the sheep. JOHN 10:11

☼ A reflection on MISSION
When I need to focus on God's will for my life

Mission statements abound in this world, but few institutions or people really live up to them. But Jesus declared that His mission statement has become reality. All that the Father has given Him to do, He has done.

Jesus did not preach to everyone in the world. He did not heal everyone, and He did not go everywhere. He didn't try to do more than He was assigned. When He ascended into heaven, there was still—and there remains today—much work to be done. But Jesus focused on the work that God had given Him to do, and He accomplished it. He didn't stray from His mission.

One day we will approach the end of our lives and stand before the Father. Will we be able to say, as Jesus did, "I brought glory to you here on earth by completing the work you gave me to do"? Is Jesus our model as we seek the will of God and minister in this world? May we be single-minded as we discern God's will for our lives and devote ourselves to accomplishing it by the power of His Spirit.

I brought glory to you here on earth by completing the work you gave me to do. JOHN 17:4

✸ A reflection on WISDOM
When I need the right perspective on my life

Wisdom is a rare commodity in our world. We have plenty of smart people, but few who are genuinely wise. True wisdom is a right understanding of the world and our role in it. It knows who God is and it knows who we are. It is a correct ordering of priorities, majoring on truth and character before superficial pleasures. It is the only way, in the long run, to be truly satisfied.

Are you satisfied with life? Do you think that the next achievement, the next salary range, the next job, the next relationship, the next "whatever" will finally make you content? Stop where you are and seek wisdom above all else. Make it your overarching priority to learn who God is, what He is like, how He relates to us, and what He is doing in this world. Then invest your entire life in what you've learned. Even if it costs you all you have, it is well worth it. Only godly wisdom can make everything else meaningful.

Getting wisdom is the wisest thing you can do! And whatever else you do, develop good judgment. PROVERBS 4:7

DAY 216

☼ A reflection on GRACE
When I need to share the Good News

The Good News is simply this—there is no condemnation
for those who are in Christ. Our sins were buried with
Him long ago. We claim this wonderful truth for ourselves; do we apply it to others? We are all dysfunctional,
though recovering; all scarred, but healed; all buried, but
raised up. No sins are held against us in this resurrection.
Any other "gospel" is not good news. Ask God to give you
a ministry of grace.

There is no judgment against anyone who believes in him.
JOHN 3:18

DAY 217

☼ A reflection on PRIDE
When I am at the end of myself

This is the amazing mercy of our God: when we get to
the helpless, hopeless end of ourselves, He is there. And
not only is He there, *He exalts us!* He lifts us up, comforts
us, and blesses us with the treasures of the Kingdom and
the gift of His Spirit. By undoing our pride, He equips us
to serve Him; and there is no greater pleasure than serving Him. There is no higher calling and no more certain
exaltation.

Those who humble themselves will be exalted. LUKE 18:14

☼ A reflection on INSUFFICIENCY
When I can't do it on my own

The disciples are astounded when Jesus says it is difficult for the rich to inherit salvation. They wonder who,
then, can be saved. But since we're all saved the same way,
through faith in Jesus, what makes it harder for the rich?
A sense of self-sufficiency. It is an obstacle to God's work
in anyone's life. In laying down this principle of salvation,
Jesus is giving us a principle of *any* spiritual work—it must
be all from God and not at all from us.

Are you in a place of insufficiency? Don't despair. He
brought you there because it is the only place where He
can step in and work and be acknowledged as the power
behind your victories. If you were not completely unable
to meet your own needs, you would receive credit for fulfilling them. He had to bring you face-to-face with your
inabilities in order to bring you face-to-face with His abilities. You are exactly where He wants you to be.

*Those who heard this said, "Then who in the world can be
saved?" He replied, "What is impossible for people is possible
with God."* LUKE 18:26-27

☸ A reflection on PRIORITIES
When I want to seek God's Kingdom first

One night early in Solomon's reign, God appeared to him and asked him what divine favor he wanted. Solomon asked for wisdom and knowledge, and because his heart's desire was not material but godly, God gave it all: wisdom and knowledge, plus riches, honor, victory, and more. In a sense, we have the same choice available to us.

We choose what things in life we will pursue. Do we value understanding more than wealth? If so, we are in the minority. Most people believe more money is the key to more happiness. In reality, more money means more maintenance, more details, more uncertain investments, more to manage, more headaches. Understanding, however, has the opposite dynamic. More is better. Always.

Isn't the choice God presents Solomon with remarkably similar to what Jesus taught His disciples? "Seek the Kingdom of God above all else, and live righteously, and he will give you everything you need" (Matthew 6:33). Examine the things you pursue. Make sure they are ultimately worth it.

Joyful is the person who finds wisdom, the one who gains understanding. For wisdom is more profitable than silver, and her wages are better than gold. PROVERBS 3:13-14

☀ A reflection on JOY
When I want to rejoice in God's sovereignty

Have you ever wept over your failures? It's a humbling experience to pour out your heart over grievous sins that can't be undone. The human heart never feels weaker than when it is faced with its undeniable shortcomings. But believe it or not, that's a great place to be. It is a blessed frailty to have no claim before God, no words with which to justify ourselves, no bargaining power whatsoever. When we can accept that, we can accept His provision; and there is no greater joy than His provision. It is all we need. We can lay down our stressful, painful attempts at self-sufficiency, and we can accept His sufficiency instead. What greater joy is there than to realize it all falls on His shoulders and not on ours?

Do you know God's joy? The joyless Christian is bearing burdens no human is capable of bearing. The joyful Christian has come to grips with personal weakness and accepted God's strength by casting all burdens on Him. Learn the art of casting those burdens; be joyful and be strong.

Don't be dejected and sad, for the joy of the LORD is your strength! NEHEMIAH 8:10

☼ A reflection on SPEECH
When I want my words to do good, not harm

Words are powerful. They can wound the spirit of another, often leaving permanent scars. They can sow seeds of corruption in innocent or wavering minds. They can soil good reputations, and they can foil good plans. They can carry a profound blessing, but they can also carry a powerful curse.

Is Proverbs 4:24 telling us simply to avoid vulgarities in our speech? Probably not. There are many forms of corruption and perversity: gossip, deception, mindless chatter, rumors, negativity, bitterness, insults, and more. All of these contradict the revealed truth of God. They run against the current of His will. In a very real sense, they slander and misrepresent the reality and beauty of His Kingdom and His character. So Scripture tells us to do away with irrelevant and improper speech.

Our words will carry a certain amount of power with them, whether for good or for bad. It is our responsibility to make sure they carry power that builds up rather than tears down; that reflects glory rather than corrupts the image of God; that honors truth rather than falsehood.

Avoid all perverse talk; stay away from corrupt speech.
PROVERBS 4:24

☼ A reflection on DEPENDENCE
When I need to rely wholly on God

Every one of our days should begin with a "declaration of dependence." We should start each morning with an emphatic acknowledgment: "Lord, I am insufficient in everything I will encounter today. I have insufficient wisdom to make the decisions I'll be required to make. I have insufficient strength to resist the temptations I'll face. I have insufficient skills to manage the conflict that may arise. I have insufficient resources to minister to the people I'll encounter. I am entirely dependent on You."

The blessing of the gospel is that in our insufficiency, Jesus is sufficient. Salvation began when we recognized that our righteousness was insufficient to coexist peacefully and eternally with a holy God, and it has continued ever since into every arena of our lives. We are deficient in every meaningful way. Embrace that deficiency, and let the eternal Vine be your life.

Remain in me, and I will remain in you. For a branch cannot produce fruit if it is severed from the vine, and you cannot be fruitful unless you remain in me. JOHN 15:4

DAY 223

   When I want to pray with power

Praying "Thy will be done" is not to be a statement of resignation. It is an appropriate deferral to God's higher plan and much more. We are not only saying "not my will," we are also saying "not the enemy's will." Wherever human tendencies or a corrupt world comes into conflict with the revealed will of God, Jesus gives us a call to arms: pray for God's will to be done.

May your will be done on earth, as it is in heaven.
MATTHEW 6:10

DAY 224

✸ A reflection on THE LIGHT OF THE WORLD
   When I need to remember my real source of truth

Mankind's research and findings have discovered some elements of truth, even apart from Christ. But it must all be measured by Him. Only He may validate for us what is—and is not—light and truth. Ask yourself this: Is Jesus my only source of light? Does my view of His exclusivity measure up to His claim?

Jesus . . . said, "I am the light of the world. If you follow me, you won't have to walk in darkness, because you will have the light that leads to life." JOHN 8:12

☼ A reflection on TIME
When I realize how short my life really is

There is something deep in the human soul—something placed there by the God who created us for eternity—that tells us life is endless. It is, but there is a substantial difference between the life we live now and the life we live in eternity. Only in one can we bear fruit for the other. What we do today can have everlasting consequences as we invest in the Kingdom of God—but our time is short. God has given us an awesome privilege. We can accomplish in that moment works of such significance that they will last forever. God can change people's lives through us. He can shape our children and our spouses and our friends through us. He can feed the hungry, encourage the outcast, redeem the lost, heal the sick, cultivate worshipers, and build His Kingdom through us. But only if we're wise and have realized the brevity of our life.

We must live with an eye on the limitations of time and the certainty of death. Wisdom fills the hearts of those who can live with such perspective.

Teach us to realize the brevity of life, so that we may grow in wisdom. PSALM 90:12

☼ A reflection on FREEDOM
When I need to shed the things that are holding me in sin

Bound by strips of linen around his hands and feet, with a cloth over his face, the resurrected Lazarus hears this command immediately after Jesus calls him out of the grave: "Take off the grave clothes and let him go." Similarly, when Jesus raises us out of our sinful state of death, there is something left to do before we run free. The grave clothes must go.

What grave clothes have had us bound? Habitual sins? Guilt? The philosophies of this age? We must be free of them, and we are helpless to shed them on our own. Jesus raises us to new life, but we in the church must be in the business of "taking off grave clothes and letting people go." In bearing one another's burdens, in our fellowship with one another, we, the walking resurrected, are assisting one another in removing the remnants of death. This is the work of the fellowship of believers.

Jesus called in a loud voice, "Lazarus, come out!" The dead man came out, his hands and feet wrapped with strips of linen, and a cloth around his face. Jesus said to them, "Take off the grave clothes and let him go."
JOHN 11:43-44, NIV

☼ A reflection on HUMILITY
When I need to remember that God wants to know me

We praise our high and holy God for His power and majesty. Do we also praise Him for His humility? We can; we serve a humble God. He did not ride into this world on a gilded chariot. He was born in a stable. He left His radiant appearance to be clothed in a human body subject to temptation and pain. We are not worthy to utter His name, but He tells us to call Him Father and Friend.

Do you suffer from the illusion of an unknowable God? You know that the Bible says He is loving and forgiving, but has that really sunk into your heart? Consider the humility of God. The high and holy One is never inaccessible to someone with a contrite spirit. He encourages your intimacy with Him. He'll even wash your feet.

[Jesus] got up from the table, took off his robe, wrapped a towel around his waist, and poured water into a basin. Then he began to wash the disciples' feet, drying them with the towel he had around him. JOHN 13:4-5

☸ A reflection on RESURRECTION
When I want to testify that Jesus is alive

We have been entrusted with the greatest truth the world has ever known. At the apex of history, Christ died and was raised—the age of resurrection had begun. Sins had been forgiven through Him. This is an incomparable story; no man-made religion has ever come close to matching it. No others have claimed resurrection to back up their teaching. The disciples, as witnesses, were entrusted as guardians of this truth.

We, too, are witnesses of the Resurrection. We haven't seen it in the same way the disciples did, but we have certainly witnessed it, if Jesus lives within us by faith. And like them, we have been radically changed by this resurrection. No one who has encountered the risen Christ can remain the same; we are compelled by His Spirit within us—His relentlessly searching Spirit—to go and tell.

It was written long ago that the Messiah would suffer and die and rise from the dead on the third day. It was also written that this message would be proclaimed in the authority of his name to all the nations, beginning in Jerusalem: "There is forgiveness of sins for all who repent." You are witnesses of all these things. LUKE 24:46-48

☀ A reflection on SPIRITUAL HUNGER
When I need to find contentment in God

Jesus says the hungry are blessed. Why? Because the truly hungry have given up trying to satisfy themselves with the wrong things. They've found that gratifying the senses isn't ultimately gratifying, and that pursuing meaningful relationships isn't the ultimate in meaning. They've found that all of our raging appetites are really a sad reminder that we have a deeper hunger for the eternal. That God-shaped vacuum that Pascal spoke of can only be filled with God—not possessions, not people, not places. God may freely bless us with all these things in abundance, but only *after* we've found our contentment in Him alone. He is no enemy of the things He's created, but He opposes them becoming the focus of our lives.

Those who have quenched their hunger with the things of this world have settled for empty calories; they're ultimately unsatisfied. The blessing of true hunger leads us to Jesus, the Bread of Life.

God blesses you who are hungry now, for you will be satisfied. LUKE 6:21

DAY 230

A reflection on MOTIVES
When I want to serve God with a pure heart

Do you ever wonder about your real motives for serving God? When you do something for God, are you doing it for public affirmation? Because you want to bargain with Him? From insecurity or fear? Take away the audience and see. Do you relate to Him well in private? Get behind closed doors and examine what's left in your relationship with Him. It can be a humbling experience, but it's a necessary one. And according to Jesus, it never goes unrewarded.

Give your gifts in private, and your Father, who sees everything, will reward you. MATTHEW 6:4

DAY 231

A reflection on LOVING GOD
When I want to rekindle my passion for God

Have you lost your first love—the love you had for Jesus when you first came to Him? You follow Jesus, but do you enjoy Him? Is your relationship with God stale and cold, or passionate and exhilarating? God desires our affection, not just our duty. Is He enjoying your relationship with Him? Are you? The fire of first love can be rekindled. Ask Him to ignite its flame in you.

Yet I hold this against you: You have forsaken your first love.
REVELATION 2:4, NIV

☀ A reflection on EVIL
When I need to recognize the enemy of my soul

If you have been a child of God for long, you know that evil is not a disembodied force. It is far more personal than that. Forsake all thought of evil simply as a force in this world. Recognize that there is a relentless, malicious intelligence behind all the pain you see. Some of Satan's minions know you by name. Jesus' ministry made that clear. He never cast out a problem; He cast out spirits. He held conversations with them and called them by name. You can't do that with an abstract principle.

How does that help us in our daily struggles? It brings us face-to-face with reality. When the Bible tells us to overcome evil with good, it is not speaking about abstracts. It means we are to overcome the evil one with the Good One. We have a Warrior, a Victor, a conquering King. Read the book of Revelation and see. And when all hell breaks loose against you, rely completely on Him.

We are not fighting against flesh-and-blood enemies, but against evil rulers and authorities of the unseen world, against mighty powers in this dark world, and against evil spirits in the heavenly places. EPHESIANS 6:12

☼ A reflection on COMPASSION
When I need to view other believers with God's love

Many of us expected to find holy people in God's Kingdom. We may have envisioned the church as a collection of folks who have gotten it right, who know what life is about and live it well. But if we've been there long enough, we realize that while the people are holy in Christ, they (and we) are still deeply flawed in themselves.

Jesus looked out upon the lame, the blind, the crippled, and the mute, and had compassion. He healed them and He fed them. What do we see when we look out upon the crowds that are coming to Jesus? Do we expect to find cleaner, healthier people? We will not. We will see similar crowds with similar problems—a world of infirmities laying all before His feet. How do we respond when we see the nature of the world within the walls of the church?

Jesus' followers are the walking wounded, those who have risen from death and are still removing their grave clothes. We bring our flaws to Him, and He is compassionate. We must be also.

When he saw the crowds, he had compassion on them because they were confused and helpless, like sheep without a shepherd. MATTHEW 9:36

☼ A reflection on MERCY
When I need to extend forgiveness to those around me

How do we know if we understand the mercy of God? There's an easy test: If you are the kind of person who shows mercy, you are the kind of person who has experienced mercy.

Jesus told a sobering parable to illustrate the point (see Matthew 18:22-35). A servant owed a king an impossibly huge sum of money. Not being able to pay it, the servant and his family were subject to being sold into slavery. But begging on his knees for patience, the servant drew sympathy from the king, who generously forgave the debt. But then the servant went out and demanded trivial payments from his debtors, bringing full charges against those who could not pay. Mercy had never sunk in. He had benefited from it, but he had no clue what it really meant.

Human nature is hypocritical. We regard others' offenses much more highly than our own. Don't buy into that double standard. Take this test: Are you judgmental toward others? Easily offended? Go back to the Cross and meditate on the forgiveness God has given you. It will cure you of any lack of mercy.

God blesses those who are merciful, for they will be shown mercy. MATTHEW 5:7

☀ **A reflection on TRUST**
When I want to depend on God alone

Those of us who claim a relationship with God have placed our trust in Him. But few of us have learned to trust the Lord *alone*. We usually trust the Lord *and* financial resources, medical research, counselors' advice, popular opinion, or any number of other things. None of these in themselves are necessarily false helps. The issue is our heart attitude of trust. Do we know in our hearts where our help really comes from? It comes from God.

Pure trust hangs everything on an invisible God. It does not hedge its bets but believes that God, as He is revealed in His Word, will act toward us as we have been told He will. In the end, it is the safest trust there is. God has never failed anyone who has invested all hopes in Him.

How pure is your trust? Are you using God to fill in the gaps around your other sources of help? If so, do not expect the blessedness of being abandoned to Him. That only comes with a pure, unbridled faith in God alone. Make the Lord your exclusive trust, and expect to be blessed.

Oh, the joys of those who trust the LORD. PSALM 40:4

☀ A reflection on PRIORITIES

When I want my love for God to be central in my life

Jesus' words in Matthew 10—that if we love our family more than we love Him, we're not worthy of Him—are startling. And in a sense we can dismiss them with a disclaimer: "None of us is worthy of Him anyway; that's why we call it grace." Acknowledging our universal unworthiness, we can move on without dealing with this radical call. But we must linger at these words longer if we really want to know the mind of Christ.

When we consider these verses in the context of the whole Bible, we know that Jesus does not oppose love for family. Rather, He opposes disproportionate love—that which depreciates His desire to have us love Him wholeheartedly. He can have no rivals in our hearts, not even good ones. In reality, He is more valuable than any other person or thing in all of existence. He is where true worth lies. When we value others more, we are not living in truth.

If you love your father or mother more than you love me, you are not worthy of being mine; or if you love your son or daughter more than me, you are not worthy of being mine.
MATTHEW 10:37

☼ A reflection on TRUTH
When I think of Jesus' mission

Jesus came into the world to testify to the truth. Think about it—infinite truth in a finite body; an answer to questions the philosophers have asked for centuries: Why are we here? Who made us? Where are we going? In Jesus, God pulled back the curtain and made divine mysteries visible. He opened the window on all that has been going on behind the scenes in this drama we call life. The Incarnation gave us truth—in person.

I was born and came into the world to testify to the truth.
JOHN 18:37

DAY 238

☼ A reflection on POWER
When I want the greatness of God to be seen in my life

Do not be satisfied with a powerless faith. It is not consistent with the teachings of Jesus, who said that if we believe in Him, we will do even greater works than He did. Ask Jesus to demonstrate this promise in you. The work of God is not limited by our concept of weak human flesh. The potential is amazing. Ask God to let you see it.

I tell you the truth, anyone who believes in me will do the same works I have done, and even greater works, because I am going to be with the Father. JOHN 14:12

☀ A reflection on LOVING OTHERS
When I find myself not caring about others

The question "Who is my neighbor?" was asked by an expert in the Law wanting to narrow his responsibility in the eyes of the Lord. If only a few are really neighbors, then only a little is required when God says to love our neighbor. He was looking for a reduction in the requirement, an easier way out.

We often do the same thing. We want God to define for us the limits of our love and compassion and mercy. But God will not define limits for our love because His love has no limits. He does choose to judge people, of course, but, unlike ours, His judgments are righteous and untainted by sin. Only He knows the right time for them. The vastness of His compassion, however, is enough to cover every person on the planet, and He calls us to be like Him. That means loving in the extreme, forgiving in the extreme, and sacrificing in the extreme. Can we do that? No. But He can do that in us and through us.

Let Him live in you without limits. Let Him open your eyes to a world of neighbors.

The man wanted to justify his actions, so he asked Jesus, "And who is my neighbor?" LUKE 10:29

☼ A reflection on TRUE GREATNESS
When I need to follow Jesus' example of service

At His last Passover dinner, Jesus took off His respectable clothes and wrapped Himself in a servant's towel. He washed what, in a semi-arid climate and a pedestrian culture, would be the dirtiest part of the human body. There is nothing glorious about cleaning feet. Jesus spotted the dirtiest, most thankless area of physical need for the disciples and met it as an illustration of His mission. Then He got up and told the disciples that they should behave in exactly the same way.

How often do we consciously perform acts of service that others consider unworthy of their talents? How often do we approach the needs of this world with a self-emptying attitude that will stoop as low as those needs demand? It goes against our human nature, doesn't it? We're always striving to work our way up, not work our way down. But Jesus' example might lead us in another direction—farther down. Toward less glory. With less recognition. According to the Savior, that's the way to greatness in God's Kingdom.

I have given you an example to follow. Do as I have done to you. JOHN 13:15

☼ A reflection on FOLLOWING JESUS
When Jesus is calling me to fully depend on Him

When Jesus calls us to follow Him, He always pushes us beyond our experience and beyond our abilities. Peter had been fishing all night with no results when Jesus' instruction came to go out into deep water. All of Peter's intuition told him that the exercise would be fruitless. But Jesus doesn't call us to do the same things we've always done in the same ways we've always done them. He puts us in places where we must depend entirely on Him.

Next time you feel helpless in a situation and know you're in over your head, remember the sovereign Lord who placed you there. He is Lord of the wind and the waves, the harvest, the loneliness, or whatever else might face us "in the deep."

Jesus knows what it takes to bear fruit—and it always involves going beyond our own expertise, our limited vision, and our resources. He calls us to launch out further and deeper, into places where we have no choice but to depend on His instructions and His power.

[Jesus] said to Simon, "Now go out where it is deeper, and let down your nets to catch some fish." LUKE 5:4

☼ A reflection on OBEDIENCE

When I need to consider how completely I submit to God

Obedience is an elusive issue for us. We are obedient to the Word up to a point, which, in effect, means we are not obedient at all. Obedience "up to a point" is ultimately disobedience; it demonstrates that we hold some masters to be higher than the Lord. We can create the illusion of obedience by doing everything right until doing right conflicts with our convenience. But when convenience supersedes obedience, we discover what rules us.

We must be careful of our own capacity for deceiving ourselves. We like to think we are obedient to God. But once in a while, He puts His finger on something that conflicts with our discipleship. Perhaps we commit to give to the Kingdom of God, but a more urgent financial obligation arises. Perhaps we're fasting, but an important dinner invitation comes our way. We must decide who our real master is. Jesus tells us we will be blessed— utterly happy and favored—if we adhere to the Word of God in such times. Then we, like Jesus, will be children who honor Him.

Blessed are all who hear the word of God and put it into practice. LUKE 11:28

⚙ **A reflection on SUFFERING**

When I need compassion for those imprisoned by their circumstances

At any given time, many of God's saints are in prison. The prison may be literal, or it may be any constraining situation such as financial debt, a broken relationship, or a physical ailment. We should never look at our imprisoned brothers and sisters and assume that God has not favored them. God's prisons are full of His loved ones. In fact, most of those whom He has used in powerful ways—such as Paul, Joseph, or John the disciple—have experienced an imprisonment, captivity, or loneliness ordained directly by Him.

Do your circumstances make you feel as if you are in prison? Don't despair; it will not last. It is designed either for your current witness or future usefulness. God is refining you and molding you into His image. Do you know someone in prison? Do not condemn. It is never God's intention for His church to turn on its visibly fallen. Pray for those who suffer and meet their needs however you can.

Remember those in prison, as if you were there yourself. Remember also those being mistreated, as if you felt their pain in your own bodies. HEBREWS 13:3

DAY 244

☼ **A reflection on CONTENTMENT**
When I need to focus on my blessings

Human beings tend to be caught in one of two cycles: a downward cycle of disappointment, or an upward cycle of blessing. When we focus on unmet needs, we lose sight of God's goodness and we are unprepared to receive more of it. When we focus on our blessings, not only do we feel more content, we actually receive the greater blessing of knowing God. He is happy to give it to those who acknowledge Him faithfully.

Happy are those who hear the joyful call to worship,
for they will walk in the light of your presence, LORD.
PSALM 89:15

DAY 245

☼ **A reflection on SCRIPTURE**
When I'm doubting some of the truths of God's Word

We need to explore the truth of God's Word and let it be written into our hearts. Do not be discouraged when you encounter verses that have not been realized in your own life. Trust that they will be. Be patient, have constant faith in God, and you will eventually see the promises as facts. God's value system will prevail, and His light will penetrate all darkness. Those who hold to His Word will be vindicated in the end.

The word of the Lord remains forever. 1 PETER 1:25

☼ A reflection on THE PERSON OF JESUS
When I am trying to understand who He really is

Jesus was an enigma. He came into this world as the child of a working-class family from a notably unnoteworthy region of the country. He amazed people with His teaching and His miracles, but He always defied their expectations. When they expected Him to act like an average Galilean, He wouldn't. When they expected Him to act like a king, He wouldn't. No one could get a handle on exactly who He was.

The same is true for us today. The God-man, the Creator incarnate, defies our expectations as well. We pray to Him as our King, but He often leads us in the way of true humanity. Then we follow Him as a human example, but He often insists on His kingly authority in our lives. He is not just our teacher, but our Lord. And He is not just our God, but our friend. He simultaneously fulfills our deepest needs for human fulfillment and for intimacy with the holy. He is exactly the answer to everything we didn't know we wanted.

You say I am a king. Actually, I was born and came into the world to testify to the truth. JOHN 18:37

☼ A reflection on DOING GOOD
When I encounter an offensive person

Surely Jesus means for us to resist evil. We are encouraged—even commanded—at several points in Scripture to stand firm against the evil one. So what does He mean when He tells us in the Sermon on the Mount not to resist an evil person? He means that when people confront us, we are to counter evil with good (Romans 12:21). Mercy triumphs over judgment (James 2:13, NIV). Evil aggression is never defeated by an evil response.

What is your reaction to evil and offensive people? No, God does not tell you to be a doormat. He does, however, tell you to demonstrate a goodness that surpasses anything this world has known. Give evil people a glimpse of heaven and do more than what is right. Do not fall to their level; we were born from a much higher source. Let them see it and be amazed.

You have heard the law that says the punishment must match the injury: "An eye for an eye, and a tooth for a tooth." But I say, do not resist an evil person! If someone slaps you on the right cheek, offer the other cheek also.
MATTHEW 5:38-39

☀ A reflection on POSSESSIONS
When I am tempted to cling to material things

In Jesus' code of ethics, there is no room for a desperate attachment to possessions. He never says we can't have them, but by example and by His teaching we learn that they are never to get in the way of our discipleship. No material possession is worth sacrificing the display of God's kind of grace.

Things are temporary. We can be unattached to them because they offer us nothing we don't already have. We can't take them with us when we go, and we wouldn't want to. They will pale in comparison to the treasures that have already been laid up for us in Christ. When a situation compels you to choose between demonstrating grace to another or maintaining your grip on your things, which do you choose? We must decide which is more important to us: a defense of our physical possessions on earth, or a demonstration of the Kingdom of God.

If you are sued in court and your shirt is taken from you, give your coat, too. . . . Give to those who ask, and don't turn away from those who want to borrow.
MATTHEW 5:40, 42

☀ A reflection on FORGIVENESS
When I need a reminder of God's mercy

Jesus told a young man who was brought to him for healing, "Your sins are forgiven." He says the same thing to us. Wherever we are, this verse redirects us. Whether we come to Jesus under deep conviction for our sin or for something we think is a greater need, this is the best thing He could say. If we have a hard time forgiving ourselves for repeated offenses toward God—even though we have confessed and heard His forgiveness—we are at odds with Jesus. We need to see ourselves as He does—clean. However, if we come to Him with a casual attitude toward sin and what we perceive as a greater request, we are also at odds with Jesus. Then, too, we must see ourselves as He does—needy.

Do Jesus' words convict you? If so, let them; that was what He wanted you to hear. Do they comfort you? If so, let them; that, too, was what He wanted you to hear.

They lowered the sick man on his mat down into the crowd, right in front of Jesus. Seeing their faith, Jesus said to the man, "Young man, your sins are forgiven."
LUKE 5:19-20

⚙ A reflection on GLORIFYING GOD
When I consider God's purposes, not my own

When crisis first hits, it's all about us. We wonder how we will be affected, how we can get out of it, how we will survive. But if we're living God-centered lives, our prayers should turn quickly to a greater cause than the immediate impact on ourselves. Our prayers should be all about God and His purposes.

When you pray for God's help, what is your motivation? If you're average and normal, you pray for your own needs. There's nothing biblically wrong with that. But there is a maturity that needs to develop. Biblical prayers must eventually fall in line with the biblical agenda: displaying the glory of God. There is no better way to gain victory in crisis than to shift our focus from our purposes to God's. Our prayers must move from "Lord, defend my cause" to "Lord, defend Your cause." The cries for help that begin with our own desperation must end with a deep concern for the work of God and the reputation of His name. Our cause must give way to His and our will must be shaped like His, for the glory of His name.

Arise, O God, and defend your cause. PSALM 74:22

DAY 251

☼ A reflection on REPUTATION
When I want my character to bring glory to God

You may work for an employer, but the impression you make on him or her is entirely God's business. He is zealous for the reputation of His name. If you have claimed His name, He is zealous for your reputation. Your character and His go hand in hand. If other people observe godly qualities in you, then God is glorified. If they don't, He isn't. We represent Jesus wherever we are, including the workplace. Represent Him with all your heart.

Work willingly at whatever you do, as though you
were working for the Lord rather than for people.
COLOSSIANS 3:23

DAY 252

☼ A reflection on SUBMISSION
When I remember that God's will is what's best for me

Are you convinced that God's will is in your best interest? The Christian life will be a struggle until we know deep down in our hearts that His commands—even the hard ones—are ultimately for our benefit. Our happiness is deeper when we listen to Him. In that sense, it is a self-fulfilling act to forsake our own will and submit to His. When we serve Him, we serve ourselves. Believe that wholeheartedly, and see what happens.

If you cling to your life, you will lose it, and if you let your
life go, you will save it. LUKE 17:33

☼ A reflection on LIVING FOR THE ETERNAL
When I need to lose my life

Most of us are self-oriented, always looking for "the next thing." The next job, the next paycheck, the next big event, the next relationship, the next purchase—we are on an endless track toward improving our lives. Yet Jesus calls His followers to give up their lives. Those who are wise will focus on "the last thing"—God's Kingdom and the reign of His Son as Lord over all.

We can't live both for now and for eternity. Many of our decisions will compel us to choose one or the other. We can't acquire expensive possessions *and* invest the cost of those possessions toward something eternal, or waste time *and* invest that time in eternal work. We can enjoy His bounty, but we will be much happier if we realize what makes for a bountiful eternity. How do we do that? We stop trying to "save" our lives and we lose them. Take your focus off "the next thing" and invest in "the last thing"—the Kingdom of God.

If you try to hang on to your life, you will lose it. But if you give up your life for my sake, you will save it.
MATTHEW 16:25

☼ A reflection on THE BODY OF BELIEVERS
When I need to value my spiritual family

"Blood is thicker than water," the saying goes. The assumption is that our deepest human loyalties lie with our blood relatives. But this is not so in the Kingdom of God. The Spirit is thicker than blood in the Kingdom. The covenant of the Kingdom ties us together in ways that genetics never will.

There is a wonderful illustration of this in the Old Testament. In marriage, man and woman leave father and mother and cleave to one another. In God's plan, the bonds of covenant take priority over the bonds of blood kinship.

Over and over again, Jesus calls His disciples to place their relationships in the Spirit above their relationships in the flesh. Our ties to Christian brothers and sisters are infinitely more substantial than those to our blood relatives. We gain hundreds of brothers, sisters, mothers, fathers, and children in the Spirit because the Spirit is thicker than blood. We are bound together with Christ, and through Christ to one another. May we glory in the family that is now ours.

Anyone who does the will of my Father in heaven is my brother and sister and mother! MATTHEW 12:50

☼ A reflection on THE HOLY SPIRIT
When I want God to control my life

Is your life driven by the Spirit? Not if it is predictable and reasonable. Not if the unbelieving world can explain it. There is considerable contrast between the ways of human nature and the ways of the Spirit. Read of the believers in Acts or of the faithful in Hebrews 11. There is an eternal wisdom behind the values Jesus preached. There is a heavenly city being built for those who shed their earthly ambitions.

Beware of a way of life that is acceptable to conventional, human reasoning. Kingdom values are a mystery to those who have fixed their gaze on this world. The mind of sinful humanity neglects the eternal for the temporal and the holy for the profane. Its followers, therefore, give tainted advice. Do not follow it. Live a supernatural life under supernatural guidance. Be blown by God's Spirit. He blows wherever He pleases and takes us where the world cannot go.

The wind blows wherever it wants. Just as you can hear the wind but can't tell where it comes from or where it is going, so you can't explain how people are born of the Spirit.
JOHN 3:8

☼ A reflection on RELYING ON CHRIST
When I need to depend only on God

Our natural tendency is to try hard, study diligently, and train ourselves to be the disciples we were meant to be. But when we use all this self-effort to attain our own growth, we quickly find ourselves feeling like failures. We come to a startling conclusion: only Jesus can live the Christian life; we can't.

Much of the Christian life is God stripping us of our self-effort so that He can live His life in us without our interference. We stress and strain over our discipleship, but God is after our trust in His strength. When we find ourselves in circumstances that are beyond our control, we are to realize our weakness and rely on His strength. God often places us in situations in which we are over our heads in order to teach us this. He must break us of self-reliance. We are never to depend on our own strength and strategies. We are to be utterly dependent on the power of God that works in us and in our circumstances.

I am the vine; you are the branches. Those who remain in me, and I in them, will produce much fruit. For apart from me you can do nothing. JOHN 15:5

✺ A reflection on KNOWING GOD
  *When I need to stop everything else and sit at
  Jesus' feet*

We are called to serve God. Yet nowhere in the Bible are
we told to serve Him at the expense of knowing Him.
Having made us for Himself, He does not primarily fashion us for usefulness. He fashions us for knowing Him. He
is first and foremost an Artist, a Craftsman, and a Father
who enjoys His children. He is not a factory worker manu-
facturing a product.

What is God's view toward you? Is He only after your
usefulness? No, the Artist wants to enjoy His work. He
seeks satisfaction in His technique and creativity—pro-
cesses that continue on in your life every day. He will use
you well, but not before He has enjoyed your company.

What is God's will for you? Jesus' words to Martha—
telling her to stop working, sit down, and listen—give us
deep insight into His heart. He first wants us at His feet.
Above all, He wants us to learn from Him.

*The Lord said to her, "My dear Martha, you are worried
and upset over all these details! There is only one thing worth
being concerned about. Mary has discovered it, and it will
not be taken away from her."* LUKE 10:41-42

DAY 258

☼ **A reflection on APPROVAL**
When I need to remember that human affirmation is not my goal

God commands us to resist the urge to run with the crowd. It's an urge based on insecurity, rooted in our former alienation from our Creator. But once reconciled to Him, we have no need for human approval. There is no culture to accommodate, no hoops to jump through for the momentary applause of a fickle audience. Best of all, there is no snare to fall into. Living Godward lives, we are kept safe from false values.

Fearing people is a dangerous trap, but trusting the LORD means safety. PROVERBS 29:25

DAY 259

☼ **A reflection on LORDSHIP**
When I need to give myself wholly to Jesus

Is Jesus Lord of 100 percent of your heart? Your thoughts, your behaviors, your dreams—are they yours or His? Jesus desires all of you. This seems like painful surrender to us, but from His perspective, it is a happy day when one of His people lays it all on the altar. He is trustworthy with everything we give Him, and He will manage our lives better than we ever have. At no point resist Him; set Him apart as Lord.

You must worship Christ as Lord of your life.
I PETER 3:15

☼ A reflection on MERCY
When I want to pay it forward

As believers, we have accepted God's mercy. But when it leads us to righteousness, we complacently forget our constant need for the mercy we once accepted. And we forget that whenever God lets us experience His character, we are to assume that character and demonstrate it to others. God shows Himself to unbelievers through the church. But if the church doesn't act like Him, how will unbelievers see Him?

The person who has encountered God's grace—really, deeply experienced it—will show it. We find that we who have been judged and forgiven have no basis for judging anyone. We discover that while the world operates on principles of pettiness and payback, the ground of God's Kingdom is mercy. Everything turns upside down. Or right-side up.

Has God's mercy made you more merciful? Jesus says the merciful will be blessed (Matthew 5:7). They are to be envied and admired. Why? They get it. They understand. They have tasted the sweetness of mercy, and they invite others to the banquet where it is served.

Her sins—and they are many—have been forgiven, so she has shown me much love. But a person who is forgiven little shows only little love. LUKE 7:47

☼ A reflection on WISDOM
When I need to ask God for insight

Why would God set up a process for us to gain wisdom? Why would He not just give it to us? Because asking for His wisdom and receiving it brings us into relationship with Him. The wisdom we receive is not information imparted, but character learned. We observe who He is, we learn to behave like Him, and we come to know Him better in the process.

Have you found yourself needing guidance in a given situation? Our usual tendency is to pray for direction, but God has a better way. Pray for wisdom, and the direction will become clear. If we were to pray for direction, God could only answer by giving us information. But if we pray for wisdom, God answers by giving us His own mind. Far from being a onetime request in a moment of need, this can be an ongoing process. God's provision of His mind is more than instructions for a way to go; it is training for a way of life.

If you need wisdom, ask our generous God, and he will give it to you. He will not rebuke you for asking. JAMES 1:5

☼ A reflection on GOD'S IMAGE
When I consider that I am made to be like Him

No one can live wisely and with purpose without realizing where we came from, where we are going, and why it all came about in the first place. We must know: we are created from Him, for Him, and in His likeness. We get caught up in jobs, mortgages, family business, relationships, and pastimes, trying to find some sense of fulfillment in all of them. But we have a higher calling lying underneath it all. *We are made to be like Him!* That's the point of it all.

Adam and Eve were modeled after Him; but we are even inhabited by Him. We are daily being conformed to the image of God in Christ (2 Corinthians 3:18). Do you live with that awareness? Are your mundane, daily decisions made with that in mind? Meditate on this amazing truth daily and let it guide your life. Whatever your other desires, there is no higher calling than this. It's what we were made for.

God created human beings in his own image. In the image of God he created them; male and female he created them.
GENESIS 1:27

☼ A reflection on TRIALS
When I want to be refined through my difficulties

Just as the Cross of Jesus revealed the character of God within Him, so does the fire of trial reveal the character of God within us. Are we patient? We and the world will know it only if our patience is tested. Are we loving? It will not be seen until we are confronted with hatred. Are we full of faith? There's no evidence until circumstances dictate against it.

Every fruit of the Spirit is latent within us until its antithesis appears. Superficial joy and real joy look exactly the same until the storm comes and blows one of them away. Peace isn't really peace unless it can survive when attacked. And deeper still, your life in the Spirit isn't life at all if it melts away when death threatens. Nothing God gives us is proven genuine until it is assaulted by the troubles of this world. It is the only way to come forth as gold. Are you running from tests? Don't. Stand firm in them. Let God do His purifying work. Get ready to shine.

When he tests me, I will come out as pure as gold.
JOB 23:10

⚙ **A reflection on MIRACLES**
When I need to act in faith

The great works of God that come about through our faith usually do not come without an initial offering from us. The offering may be pitifully small—so much the better to display God's power—but it still must be given. Every miraculous work begins with an act of faith, a stepping out of God's people on the limb of trust. In handing the five loaves and two fishes to Jesus, the disciples were not for a moment thinking this human effort would meet the needs of the crowd; they were only giving what they had. That's where miracles begin.

Our abilities are too paltry to meet the overwhelming needs of this world. But when Jesus gets through with them, they are powerfully sufficient. Do we want Him to work through us? We must give Him what we have.

The disciples came to him and said, "This is a remote place, and it's already getting late. Send the crowds away so they can go to the villages and buy food for themselves." But Jesus said, "That isn't necessary—you feed them." "But we have only five loaves of bread and two fish!" they answered. "Bring them here," he said. MATTHEW 14:15-18

☸ A reflection on DIRECTION
When I need God's guidance

Do you need direction? Guidance? Wisdom from above?
The crucial step, often neglected, is to ask for it. How
often we try to figure things out on our own! How often
we ask others for advice before we ask God! Ask Him now.
Ask often. Make the asking a regular part of your life.
Don't wait until trouble comes; learn the mind of God
now. He offers it generously.

*If you need wisdom, ask our generous God, and he will give
it to you. He will not rebuke you for asking.* JAMES 1:5

DAY 266

☸ A reflection on PEACE
When I am looking for security in my life

Where do you look for your sense of peace? A bank
account? An education? The national defense? Standard
airbags? Our trust in wealth or walls can be a veiled statement of mistrust in God. He must let our false securities
fail before our trust turns back to Him. Let yourself trust
the One who is unfailingly trustworthy. Accept no substi-
tutes. Rest in His sovereign arms.

*If I have put my trust in gold or said to pure gold, "You
are my security," . . . I would have been unfaithful to
God on high.* JOB 31:24, 28, NIV

☼ A reflection on CRISIS
When a situation appears disastrous

The young Jesus was missing for three days, a painfully long time for a mother and father who don't know where their child is. It wasn't the only time Jesus would be missing for three days. Both times—when He calmly sat in the Temple discussing theology and when He lay in the grave—His loved ones were thrown into a panic. Yet both times, Jesus calmly gives reassurance. *Faith is the appropriate response*, He seems to imply in His gentle rebukes. God remains on His throne, Jesus is Lord, and the situation at hand—whatever it is—isn't nearly as critical as it seems.

Isn't that an accurate portrayal of our reaction and His response in a crisis? We often run around in a panic because a given situation isn't quite what we planned, or perhaps it even appears disastrous. All the while, Jesus calmly awaits our discovery that God is in fact sovereign, and Jesus Himself does in fact remain Lord. Are you in a crisis? Hear Him asking, "Why were you searching for Me?" and know that your situation is much larger to you than it is to Him.

"Why did you need to search?" he asked. "Didn't you know that I must be in my Father's house?" LUKE 2:49

❋ A reflection on REPENTANCE
When I am confronted with my sins

What do you do when confronted with your sins? Do you get defensive? Are you resistant? That may depend on the one who is pointing out your sins. A friend's rebuke is hard to take, a stranger's harder still. The Bible rebukes us frequently, but we find it easy to ignore the Word when we want to. After all, there are lots of pages to turn to when we want a more uplifting, encouraging thought. Regardless of where the rebuke comes from, we don't usually want to be bothered with messages about our own corruption. We'd rather dwell on how far we've come than how far we have to go. We don't like reminders that no matter how long we've been disciples, we are in need of great mercy.

Test your level of "repentability." Evaluate your response when you are confronted with your sin, either by another person or by the Word of God. Take your cues from David, whose response to his sin was grief. Let humility be your guide, and see the mercy of God.

Then David confessed to Nathan, "I have sinned against the LORD." 2 SAMUEL 12:13

☼ A reflection on GOD'S OMNIPRESENCE
When I realize that God sees everything about me

Whatever we do, whatever deep motives prompt us to do it, wherever we go, and the reasons we go there, God sees. He knows our every impulse, whether good or bad. He has seen it all. That is more than a little disarming, but there is also great comfort in knowing about this all-seeing God. Why? Because once we realize that He sees us as we truly are, and understand that He has offered us this wonderful invitation to be saved and loved by Him *anyway*, we can relax in utter security. He has seen our worst, and it has not sent Him running in the other direction. He still pursues us. He still asks for our fellowship. He sees all, and it's okay.

There is no fooling God—our acting ability is not that good. The best relationship with Him is an honest one. He learns nothing new by our honesty, but we cannot learn anything about Him without it. When we drop the pose, we find our security in Him rather than in our image. We know His love must be deep; He loves *us*!

The LORD is watching everywhere, keeping his eye on both the evil and the good. PROVERBS 15:3

☼ A reflection on BLESSING
When I wonder if God really wants to bless me

God is a blesser by nature. He gave us life. He gave us a beautiful creation. He sustains our every moment of existence. We've rebelled and corrupted it all, yet His response is merciful. Through miracle after miracle, He brought His people into a saving relationship with Him, and He has demonstrated His commitment throughout the millennia to continue saving. And yet we still think He might be reluctant to hear us in our hour of need.

This is what sin does to people: it corrupts our understanding of God. We come to see Him as a distant Sovereign who only rarely grants us His favor. We think He is reluctant to grace us with His gifts when, in fact, He constantly gives us His grace. God blesses. Lavishly. Far beyond our comprehension. It's who He is.

We pray without faith—and therefore without much result—when we start with a lesser view of God. The one who comes to God with the assumption that He blesses will find that He actually does.

If you sinful people know how to give good gifts to your children, how much more will your heavenly Father give good gifts to those who ask him. MATTHEW 7:11

☼ A reflection on THE POOR

When I need to develop compassion for the less fortunate

For most of us, caring for the poor is an afterthought. We're not unconcerned; we're just not very intentional about our efforts. But for God, caring for the poor is essential. It is an emphatic theme in His Word. It is written into His Law, it is measured by the prophets, it is characteristic of Jesus, and it is a substantial ministry in the New Testament church. From cover to cover, the Bible tells us of God's concern for the poor. And our view of the needy reflects our view of God; we need to see in the destitute the image of God.

Why is it so important to God that we be kind to the needy? Because if we aren't, we've forgotten who we are. We were needy. He was kind. Did we learn anything from His example? Do we consider His love valuable only because it was applied to us? Did mercy really sink in? The poor remain because God wants to know: How much do you value His ways? Give Him a demonstration today. Show kindness to those who need it most.

Those who oppress the poor insult their Maker, but helping the poor honors him. PROVERBS 14:31

☼ A reflection on BEING RENEWED
When I want to put on my new nature

Are you reluctant to place both feet firmly in the Kingdom of God? Do you try to hang on to remnants of your former citizenship? Let them go. The way to advance in your new Kingdom is to be reclothed in your new nature. It's a daily process of denying deceitful desires and saturating ourselves in a new attitude. We become like God in righteousness and holiness. There is no greater wisdom than this.

Throw off your old sinful nature and your former way of life. . . . Put on your new nature, created to be like God—truly righteous and holy. EPHESIANS 4:22, 24

DAY 273

☼ A reflection on GOD'S DIRECTION
When I am resolved to obey God's wisdom

God's direction is always the right one. When He speaks, there is no better option. Do you ask God for His wisdom with a resolve to obey it? If not, do not expect it to come. But if your heart will commit to His way, His way will be easily found. God gives us His mind in response to our faith.

When you ask him [for wisdom], be sure that your faith is in God alone. Do not waver, for a person with divided loyalty is as unsettled as a wave of the sea that is blown and tossed by the wind. JAMES 1:6

❋ A reflection on JESUS' BIRTH
When I wonder why Jesus came

When we think of the Christmas story, we usually think of the birth narratives in Matthew and Luke that explain how Jesus came into this world. But why did Jesus come? One of the answers is given in Matthew 5:17, where Jesus says He came to accomplish the purpose of the Law and the Prophets. These two things are the Word of God—immutable and inviolable. Only by man fulfilling them can man be saved.

How could God accomplish our salvation in light of our numerous willful violations? He sent a Man—Jesus—to fulfill all righteousness. Jesus did not come to tell us "never mind" about the law; God has never just ignored our offenses. Jesus came as a law fulfiller. He paid attention not only to every small letter and stroke of the pen, but also to the Spirit behind them. In doing so, He accomplished what we could not—righteousness—and then He gave it to us. That's the reason for Christmas. The baby in the manger was our only hope to fulfill God's law. Thank God He did.

Don't misunderstand why I have come. I did not come to abolish the law of Moses or the writings of the prophets. No, I came to accomplish their purpose. MATTHEW 5:17

⚙ A reflection on PRIDE
When I need to reject the world's mind-set

Our world honors pride. We often give the most media attention to those who demand it. Athletes make arrogant claims and then are lauded for their competitiveness. Political and military leaders proudly wield their power over vulnerable people and are rewarded for their assertiveness. Making a name for oneself is an honorable business in the world's culture. We might easily be drawn into that philosophy if we don't continually remind ourselves of God's hatred for pride. It is a consistent biblical theme: pride is repulsive. It directs glory inward instead of upward. It seeks the honor of the gifted rather than the honor of the Giver. In its very essence, it ignores God. If we want to avoid it, we must always honor Him.

Let every hint of pride be repulsive to you. Let God deal with those who seek their own glory; it is not our job to humble anyone. But the Bible repeatedly tells us to humble ourselves. Agree with God that pride is a detestable thing. Send it away and seek His glory. His honor comes to those who do.

The LORD detests the proud; they will surely be punished.
PROVERBS 16:5

※ A reflection on LOVING GOD
When I want to draw closer to God

We often love Jesus because we ought to, not because we just can't help ourselves. And we *should* love Him this way. *Agape* love—that unconditional, noblest form of love by which God defines Himself and the community of His believers—is the only kind of love that stands firm when circumstances shift. But we should love Him with pleasure, too. God means to be enjoyed.

What kind of love do we have for Jesus? Is it only the *agape* love—noble and purposeful, but sometimes lacking in the warmth of friendship? Or is it the *phileo* kind of love as well—an irrepressible affection and friendship for One whose Presence we actually enjoy? If we believe in Jesus—lovingly and enthusiastically—we experience the kind of love that comes from the heart of God not only because it is *right*, but also because it is *enjoyable*. Cultivate both kinds of love. Enjoy the blessing of God's affection.

The Father himself loves you dearly because you love me and believe that I came from God. JOHN 16:27

⚙ **A reflection on THE CROSS**
When I want to experience the depths of God's wisdom

Becoming wise in the ways of the Kingdom is like putting on a set of strange, new clothes. We look different and we feel different. This is no illusion; we *are* different. And the Cross is our holy invitation to go deep. We are not saved for superficiality. Instead, we are beckoned into the wisdom that underlies the foundation of this universe, called to understand its purpose, its dynamics, its direction, and its needs. The invitation is more remarkable than we might think; it is a summons to participate in the works of God. *Never be afraid to go deep.*

The privilege of the believer is to share in the deep things of God. The Cross was a secret mystery from before the beginning of time, but now it is revealed for our glory (1 Corinthians 2:7). We are colaborers with Him, sharing in His likeness! All creation must marvel at the sight. Never be content with staying on the surface, and never assume you've learned enough. God is deeper than most people know. Dive into the depths of His wisdom.

His Spirit searches out everything and shows us God's deep secrets. I CORINTHIANS 2:10

☀ A reflection on JESUS' CALL
When I need the courage to fix my eyes on Jesus

Our experience of faith mirrors Peter's experience when he tried to walk to Jesus on the water. We hang in the balance between faith and unbelief, alternately fixing our gaze on Christ and then on the waves around us. Unfortunately, the waves frequently loom larger to us. We sometimes even obsess about this wind and these waves, which do not hesitate to tell us that we are doing the impossible—living supernatural lives. Frequently, we listen to them and we sink.

But the call of Jesus is this: "Come." We *are* to live supernatural lives. We may think we are being appropriately sensible when we measure the wind and waves and proceed with caution. But Jesus urges us to ignore them altogether and fix our eyes on Him. He alone is the true measure of our situation. When He tells us to step out on the water, *we can*, regardless of how many contrary warnings against it we have ever heard or imagined. His is the only voice we must hear.

Peter called to him, "Lord, if it's really you, tell me to come to you, walking on the water." "Yes, come," Jesus said.
MATTHEW 14:28-29

☼ A reflection on PEACE
When I need to rest in God

Paul says we are to let the peace of Christ rule in our hearts. He doesn't say peace is simply to exist in our hearts or influence our hearts periodically—it is to rule. Take this diagnostic test: are you in conflict with others? It is likely a reflection of the condition of your heart. Ask God to still your turbulent waters. Let Jesus rule in the deepest corners of your being. Know the depths of His peace.

Let the peace that comes from Christ rule in your hearts.
COLOSSIANS 3:15

DAY 280

☼ A reflection on ETERNITY
When I want to live in light of the Resurrection

As Christians, we must frequently take an inventory of our life. Are we living in light of the Resurrection? Or are we offering up our most valuable resources for a momentary benefit? To know the difference, we must be sensitive to the motivations behind our actions. Are our morals based on eternal considerations? Are we using our time, money, and talents for today alone or for the Kingdom of God? Rearrange your life, if you must. Seize the Kingdom. It lasts.

If there is no resurrection, "Let's feast and drink, for tomorrow we die!" I CORINTHIANS 15:32

☀ A reflection on TRIALS
When God is refining me

We can take comfort in the fact that God is sovereign over all our trials. Whether He is letting hardship strengthen our faith, or disciplining us for some sin, He is always the Lord of our situation. He does not train those whom He does not intend to use in wonderful ways. Though we may suffer at times, we suffer with a purpose. He has a plan for us that only this type of hardship will prepare us for.

Many times we pray to know Christ better, to have deeper fellowship with Him, and to be more fruitful in His work. We must learn that this prayer will likely result in more of the refiner's fire, more time in the training camp of His Kingdom. Should we stop praying it? Of course not. None of those who have been used mightily by God have avoided the difficult developing of their character and faith. They have been through the fiery trials and would willingly go through them again.

I correct and discipline everyone I love. So be diligent and turn from your indifference. REVELATION 3:19

☀ A reflection on SUCCESS
When I want to do well in God's eyes

What does it mean to commit to the Lord whatever we do? It doesn't mean that we come up with our own plans and then ask God to bless them. It means that if we have made a commitment to honor God with our lives, and that commitment has shaped our whole manner of living, then He will ensure success.

How does God define success? The perfect case study is Jesus. In God's eyes, crucifixion is a success. So is persecution, hardship, and sacrifice. The issue is not status, achievements, reputation, or profit. It is godly character and eternal fruit. Know what it means to commit your ways to God and understand how He defines success, and the result will be a highly successful life. It may or may not appear that way to others, but appearance seems to matter little to God. The One who sees is the One who makes the final judgment on how well you've lived. Commit to Him, and the blessing of success is assured.

Commit your actions to the LORD, and your plans will succeed. PROVERBS 16:3

⚙ A reflection on WORDS
When I want to use the power of speech wisely

Speech is an awesome responsibility. It's hard to imagine that our casual comments can have eternal implications, but they can. God anoints them for blessing, and Satan uses them for cursing. Both blessings and curses have a dramatic impact on the heart and soul of human beings.

Have you ever considered the implications of your words? They can be powerful, whether you realize it or not. Through your speech, you can set the mood of a room and cultivate the direction of a life. What comes out of your mouth will either build up or tear down. It all depends on what you say and how you say it. Try this mental exercise: Learn to consider each of your words as a powerful spark. See the implications beyond the moment. Discipline your mouth to be silent until you are sure your words are both consistent with Scripture and flavored with grace. That doesn't mean you'll never say anything harsh—some situations beg for rebuke. But let your speech be redemptive. Most of all, let it point to God.

Kind words are like honey—sweet to the soul and healthy for the body. PROVERBS 16:24

❁ A reflection on LORDSHIP
When I need to surrender to God's transformation

Many Christians make very little effort to actually apply the teachings of Jesus to their lives. We ask Him to save us but may not expect Him to transform us. We call Him "Lord" but just *know* He wouldn't challenge our innermost being. We forget that the nature of God in Christ is radically contrary to sinful human nature.

Let's not misunderstand—His lordship isn't another external law placed upon our unwilling hearts. He gets inside us. He transforms us from within. His work may be uncomfortable, but there is an overcoming—and loving—power in it.

So what is the answer to His question? Why do we call Him "Lord" and do not do what He says? Perhaps we do not know how thoroughly He plans to change us. Perhaps we do not ask Him to change us from within. Or maybe we have asked but don't really believe He can overcome our obstinacy. We know ourselves too well, and Him not enough. Understand, ask, and believe. Change is the heart of His gospel.

Why do you keep calling me "Lord, Lord!" when you don't do what I say? LUKE 6:46

⚙ A reflection on WORSHIP
When I need to center my life on exalting God

When we consider God's will for our lives, we usually are thinking in terms of a career direction or a major family or financial decision. God wants to direct us in these, but He has a higher priority. What is God's will for us? Worship.

Jesus calls for obedient followers. He asks us to pray that laborers be sent into the harvest. But above all of these callings of service is a prior calling: to worship Him in spirit and in truth. This is our ultimate purpose. When all is said and done, when the Lord has returned, when the multitudes are gathered before His throne, we will know we exist only for worship.

There is a reason Jesus pointed to our love for God as the greatest commandment (Matthew 22:36-37). It fulfills our purpose. We were designed for worship, and the Father is seeking those who know that.

The time is coming—indeed it's here now—when true worshipers will worship the Father in spirit and in truth. The Father is looking for those who will worship him that way. JOHN 4:23

☼ A reflection on MATERIALISM
When I want to keep my mind focused on the Kingdom of God

Materialism is deceptive. We are encouraged at every turn to live the high life, grab life by the horns, and hang on to what we've got. We are obsessive about our upward mobility. Our problem is that we've forgotten how to define "upward." Know your citizenship in heaven and invest in it. Take care of your physical needs and the needs of others, but live for the Kingdom of God. It will forever pay dividends.

A person is a fool to store up earthly wealth but not have a rich relationship with God. LUKE 12:21

DAY 287

☼ A reflection on GLORIFYING GOD
When I want to acknowledge God's great name

One of God's purposes behind His great works, aside from the simple fact that He loves us, is His zeal for the glory of His name. When we credit Him for what He has done, we are aligning ourselves with the zeal of the Lord Himself. We are fulfilling our created purpose: to glorify Him. Acknowledge God as the source of your blessings and give Him glory. As a result, God will be even more ready to give to you.

Give to the LORD the glory he deserves! PSALM 96:8

☀ A reflection on TRANSFORMATION
When I need to be cleansed from the inside out

A problem many of us face is that we can restrain our outward behavior while retaining all of the evil thoughts within us. When that happens, what we've changed is our appearance, not our heart. This is the condition of the Pharisee, and it's not Jesus' solution for sin.

If the problem of sin is an inward problem, it must be treated with an inward solution. What is the inward solution? The habitation of Christ Himself in our hearts by faith, and our constant, conscious reliance on Him to change us from within.

If inward change is your struggle—and you are not alone, if it is—resist the way of your human nature. Do not be content with covering the outward manifestation of an unclean heart. Invite Jesus to do an inward work, conforming your heart into His pure image—not just once, but constantly. Believe that He will, and see what happens.

It's not what goes into your body that defiles you; you are defiled by what comes from your heart. MARK 7:15

☼ A reflection on SUFFERING
When I wonder why bad things happen

It is part of human nature to ask why. We see tragedy in our world and we ask why. We encounter hardship in our lives, or suffer loss, and we ask why. We want to know the reason for it all, the unifying purpose behind this strange, needy world. Jesus reminds us: it is all for the glory of God. The universe exists to display His splendor.

It's not about us—it's about Him. By our captivity He is known as Deliverer. By our sin He is known as Savior. By our weakness He is known as powerful. Next to our hatred, His love amazes. Every evil we can think of has the potential of being a platform for the goodness of God. It's all about Him.

Do we complain about our hardships? If so, we have forgotten that the universe is meant to glorify God, not us. Consider how His power might be made known in our trials. Redirect your prayers not to improve your situation but to have your situation demonstrate His glory. Thank Him for making Himself known.

His disciples asked him, "Why was this man born blind?"
. . . Jesus answered, "This happened so the power of God
could be seen in him." JOHN 9:2-3

☼ A reflection on TRUTH
When I want to be known for integrity

Jesus calls His Spirit "the Spirit of truth." What does it mean for us that "truth" is part of one of His revealed names? It means that He will remind us of Jesus' words and teaching (John 14:26); He will guide us into all truth when we are confused and lack wisdom (16:13); and we ourselves will be known by our truthfulness, because He will infuse us with His pure, uncompromising nature.

We are stewards of truth. We cannot become casual in our portrayal of truth, whether in the minor details of life or the proclamation of the eternal gospel. We can't fudge the facts a little to make ourselves look better or to get us out of difficult circumstances; and we can't soften the truths of the gospel for a low-tolerance world. Those who are filled with His Spirit will be guided by—and always known for—uncompromising truth.

I will ask the Father, and he will give you another advocate to help you and be with you forever—the Spirit of truth.
JOHN 14:16-17, NIV

☼ A reflection on APPROVAL
When I want to be honored by people

One enduring trait of most human beings is that we obsess about the approval of others. We are, more often than we think, shaped by the opinions of those around us. And yet our lives are to be entirely God-directed. When we obsess about others' opinions, we have a distorted view of reality. We place more stock in something temporal and transient than we do in what is eternal and most worthy. We ignore the truly valuable (the will of God) to pursue an illusion (the approval of human beings). It is an incredibly costly exchange.

Jesus tells us emphatically not to fear people. He urges His followers to think only of God. In any decision we make, we are to consider His character and His plan and ignore the effect our decision might have on our standing in others' eyes. Do we fear for our self-esteem? His grace will be more than enough to compensate. We are—without compromise—to seek the esteem that comes from serving God rather than the esteem that comes from human approval. Only then will we be in touch with reality.

I'm not trying to win the approval of people, but of God.
GALATIANS 1:10

✸ A reflection on HOPE
When I am discouraged

We face a lot of discouragement in life. We hear the negative reports of those who think every situation is a hopeless one. And when we encounter "impossible" situations, we are frequently fed complex, impotent approaches to them. But we need to remember that with Jesus, no situation is hopeless. Even apparent disasters are entirely redeemable for a sovereign God who responds to faith. Let Jesus walk into your situation and speak a soothing, simple word. Let Him enter into the distresses of your life and gently take your hand.

Is it discouragement? Depression? Hopelessness? Dread? The ravages of death itself? No matter. Let Him come in, take your hand, and whisper the encouraging, life-giving words only a loving parent can whisper. We need to tune out everything else and listen to the gentle voice of our God.

The crowd laughed at him. But he made them all leave, and he took the girl's father and mother and his three disciples into the room where the girl was lying. Holding her hand, he said to her, "Talitha koum," which means "Little girl, get up!" And the girl, who was twelve years old, immediately stood up and walked around! MARK 5:40-42

☼ A reflection on PRIDE
When I need to be humbled

God can undo our pride by reminding us of our neediness. We can't relate to God properly unless we understand that all we have and all we are is by grace. When we take credit, we deny God's generosity. That is not a minor offense. His love will correct us. Wake up each morning with a self-reminder that your life is all about grace. It will keep you humble and it will open God's arms to you.

He is able to humble the proud. DANIEL 4:37

DAY 294

☼ A reflection on CONTROL
When I am anxious about a situation

Are you going through a difficult trial? Relinquish your goals in it. In your heart, transfer ownership of the situation to God. Our anxiety comes from a false sense of control—a sense that we perhaps are responsible to manipulate the crisis to work out for good. That's God's job. Be willing for Him to work it out any way He chooses. Let go of your will, and let your heart and your mind be at peace.

Don't worry about anything; instead, pray about everything. Tell God what you need, and thank him for all he has done. Then you will experience God's peace.
PHILIPPIANS 4:6-7

☀ A reflection on INTEGRITY
  When I want to be a person of truth

Dishonesty is epidemic in our culture. When we lie—even in a seemingly insignificant way—it is often because we are afraid of what will happen if we tell the truth. We do not trust God to honor our integrity. But our God is a God of integrity. It is in His character. He never lies, and He is not silent when the truth needs to be revealed. It is His nature to be absolutely reliable. There is no hint of pretense in Him. He is who He says He is, He does what He says He will do, and He honors those who follow His lead. Always.

Though we are called to be like Him, our integrity falls short of His. He is shaping us to reflect His glory, but when we give a false impression, we interfere with His work. Trust God with the truth. Tell it and display His integrity. Know that He will always defend truth—and those who tell it.

The LORD detests lying lips, but he delights in those who tell the truth. PROVERBS 12:22

☀ A reflection on CONTENTMENT
When I hunger for righteousness

God's Word often defines us by our hunger. Jesus said those who hunger and thirst for righteousness would be filled (Matthew 5:6). It pleases Him when we crave His righteousness and seek it as a treasure. The craving, by His description, is who we are. This is why Proverbs can tell us that the righteous will not go hungry—because what they hunger for is righteousness. God gives such treasures to all who seek them. The wicked, however, crave wickedness. If they are filled, it will only be for a moment; it will not last.

Does contentment elude you? Check your desires. They are an accurate description of who you are and the kingdom you'd rather live in. What do you hunger for? If your cravings lead you to God, you will never go hungry. If they do not, you always will. God's Kingdom is always about righteousness. Never forget that, and be filled.

The Lord will not let the godly go hungry, but he refuses to satisfy the craving of the wicked. PROVERBS 10:3

☀ A reflection on DIRECTION
When I need guidance for the future

Our world presents us with a multitude of options, many of which seem good, but we don't know enough about the future to make decisions well. We want more information, but we hesitate when we find that getting direction from Him means, first and foremost, getting Him. His Spirit shapes us, and His wisdom becomes a part of us.

God is not usually an oracle-giver; He's a life-transformer. He usually directs us not by passing on information about what we're to do, but by fundamentally altering us from within. He changes our character, our outlook, our priorities. Then we are directed by the person God has made us into—a new creation governed by the indwelling Jesus.

When we trust Him with all our heart, refuse to lean on our own understanding, and acknowledge His sufficiency in everything, *then* He makes our paths straight. Why? Because He is present. We have not simply used Him for His vast information, we have invited Him to come along on the journey.

Trust in the LORD with all your heart and lean not on your own understanding; in all your ways acknowledge him, and he will make your paths straight. PROVERBS 3:5-6, NIV

⚙ **A reflection on OBEDIENCE**
When I want my actions to show my love for Jesus

How reluctant our generation is to link love and obedience! We see love and commitment as two separate entities, whether the issue is marriage, friendship, or discipleship. We want to say we love Jesus even when we have no intention of obeying Him, but Jesus gives us no such option. Obedience is an indicator of what's in the heart. If we obey Him, it means we love Him. If we don't obey Him, it means we don't really love Him—not as much as our other loves, anyway.

Our hearts will be wherever our treasure is (Matthew 6:21). If our hearts are not invested in His teaching, we won't follow Him, no matter how much we try to convince ourselves that we are His disciples.

How is your obedience? Is it sporadic? Is it halfhearted? Then so is your love. You may not always be full of passionate feelings toward your Savior, but the committed kind of love will follow Him persistently, even when the feelings are not there. Jesus has already demonstrated His love. Show Him yours. Obey His teaching.

All who love me will do what I say. JOHN 14:23

☼ A reflection on APPROACHING GOD
When I am hesitant to ask Him for what I need

"You don't have what you want because you don't ask God for it," writes James (4:2). Jesus says clearly, "Everyone who asks, receives" (Matthew 7:8). In fact, many of His parables are about asking—persistent, bold, specific asking.

Jesus insists on specific requests, even though He knows all of our needs before we even ask. Perhaps He insists so we'll recognize His answer when it comes—a gift specifically from Him and specifically for us. Perhaps it is so that when the answer comes we will clearly see how His will differs from our own limited vision. Perhaps it is so we will remember, having voiced our request, to give thanks when it is granted. Perhaps the asking and receiving give witness to the world in a way that the presumption of providence would not.

We wonder sometimes why God has not met a certain need. Our first step, often neglected, is to be specific. We must ask.

"What do you want me to do for you?" Jesus asked.
MARK 10:51

DAY 300

☼ A reflection on PERSEVERANCE
When I need endurance in my circumstances

What is your reaction to trials? Do you expect instantaneous answers to your prayers for deliverance? More often than not, you will be disappointed. Change your perspective. Rather than looking for escape, look for the benefit of the trial. Let endurance have its perfect result. Ask God what He's accomplishing and then participate in it willingly. If you can learn perseverance, you will be a rarity in this world and well fit for the Kingdom of God.

You know about Job, a man of great endurance. You can see how the Lord was kind to him at the end. JAMES 5:11

DAY 301

☼ A reflection on GOD'S LOVE
When I need to remember God's faithfulness

Human nature tells us to hide when we're in trouble. God's Word tells us to cry out to Him. Following God's Word is infinitely wiser than following fallen human nature. The next time you're in distress, cling to one unalterable fact: the faithful, unfailing love of God for His redeemed.

Those who are wise will take all this to heart; they will see in our history the faithful love of the Lord. PSALM 107:43

⚙ A reflection on COMMITMENT
When I hear the call to absolute discipleship

Our society respects those who dabble in religious belief but reviles those who are wholeheartedly committed—especially if the object of commitment is Christ. In our culture it is respectable to say we are seeking, but arrogant to say we have found. Throughout history, those who have "left everything" to follow Christ have often been considered fools.

Have we come to view total commitment as an option? Or worse, is it to be avoided as an unrealistic demand? Where in Scripture does Jesus expect of His disciples anything less than total devotion? Jesus is perfectly clear in His absolute call to discipleship. We are to abandon all that we are to Him.

Lord, grant that we might not be afraid of radical commitment, even if we are ostracized by a world that doesn't understand it.

Peter said, "We've left our homes to follow you." "Yes," Jesus replied, "and I assure you that everyone who has given up house or wife or brothers or parents or children, for the sake of the Kingdom of God, will be repaid many times over in this life, and will have eternal life in the world to come."
LUKE 18:28-30

☼ A reflection on FAITH
When I consider the nature of my belief

Many times we put our faith in faith. We take Jesus' teaching about mustard seeds and mountains to mean that faith is the object we are to desire most. But we must be careful. Though Jesus is consistent and frequent in His praise of faith, He never says that faith is the end of the matter. It is not faith in our own ability to have faith that is the key to answered prayer. It is faith in *Him*.

Have you struggled to have more faith? Take your eyes off your faith and put them on God. Your understanding of God *is* your faith. Your belief will never grow larger; your view of God will. Meditate on His grandeur and you'll find yourself trusting Him more. And you'll also find that nothing is impossible.

I tell you the truth, if you had faith even as small as a mustard seed, you could say to this mountain, "Move from here to there," and it would move. Nothing would be impossible. MATTHEW 17:20

☼ A reflection on BLESSING
When I want to ask humbly for God's approval

What father would deny a son who sincerely comes to him for blessing? Not only would he bestow abundance and fullness on his son, he would do so with great excitement and joy. Blessing children is natural, even for those of us who are tainted with impurity. How much greater the blessing from the One who is pure love!

When we ask God for His blessing, do we ask with arrogance? Or do we get on our knees before the Father and humbly ask that His highest will for us be made real? Do we ask without regard to the Father's character, will, or feelings? Or do we know Him personally enough to ask with the respect He deserves?

God is a blesser by nature. Yet we often assume reluctance on His part, as though He would begrudge us anything. Not so, says Psalm 84:11—"The LORD will withhold no good thing from those who do what is right." Even when we take His goodness for granted, He often blesses. How much more joyfully He blesses when the request is honoring to Him.

If you sinful people know how to give good gifts to your children, how much more will your heavenly Father give good gifts to those who ask him. MATTHEW 7:11

☼ A reflection on JESUS' SECOND COMING
When I want to live in the knowledge that Jesus will return

Many Christians believe that Jesus is coming again but do not live with the urgency that indicates that it is a real belief. But there is a reason Jesus told His disciples to be ready and then waited more than two thousand years. He intends for us to live every day with an eternal perspective, sowing seeds that will bear everlasting fruit. He wants us to be single-minded in our service, preparing His household in the same way we would if He were standing beside us, telling us what to do. Those who love Him serve Him well. Those who give Him mere lip service will get up and act busy when He comes through the door.

Does Jesus' return guide your life today? Or is His return on the back burner, a distant thought while you live out the demands of the present? Be careful of the answer. According to Jesus, it's the difference between being wise and being foolish.

Be dressed and be ready. Keep the lamps burning. Watch for the Master's return and be wise. He is coming.

You also must be ready all the time, for the Son of Man will come when least expected. LUKE 12:40

☼ A reflection on DREAMS
When I want to turn my aspirations into reality

God gives us dreams because He wants us to accomplish things. In the heart that dreams, God can plant visions of widespread, effective ministries, of preaching the gospel and helping the poor, of finding innovative ways to build the Kingdom of Heaven. Dreams are the *beginning* of all good accomplishments—but in themselves, they don't accomplish anything. Though God plants dreams in our hearts, He does not simply leave them there. God wants our visions to have a plan of action.

Do you have a vision you're convinced God has given you? If so, what are your plans? God is expecting you to take the dreams He has given you and move them forward. First write the steps down; then take them. Are you unsure of your dreams? Still trying to determine whether they are self-ordained or God-given? Then ask God specifically to encourage the ones that are also His dreams for you. But once know the difference, don't let them sit. Ask for His timing. Ask for His wisdom. And act on His promises.

A hard worker has plenty of food, but a person who chases fantasies has no sense. PROVERBS 12:11

※ A reflection on OBEDIENCE
When I need to let the Word affect my actions

Listening to the Word is immensely profitable, but it can be dangerously deceptive as well. When we hear the Word, we often make the mistake of believing it has become a part of our lives. That's an illusion. The Word is only effective when we've allowed God to move it from our minds into our hearts, and then outward into our actions. Anything else will lull us into a false sense of security. Do not be deceived. "Do what it says."

Don't just listen to God's word. You must do what it says.
JAMES 1:22

※ A reflection on MERCY
When I want to show compassion

Those who have regard for the weak always have God's sympathetic ear. In His mercy, God cares for our needs regardless of our level of compassion. But He cares for them more readily, more powerfully, and more demonstrably if we have demonstrated His nature toward others. Do we withhold grace? Then grace will be hard to find. Or are we examples of mercy? If so, we will have mercy in abundance.

Oh, the joys of those who are kind to the poor! The LORD rescues them when they are in trouble. PSALM 41:1

☼ A reflection on KNOWING GOD
When I need to reflect on God, my Treasure

Jesus told His disciples that they were blessed beyond measure by knowing Him. They were in a privileged place. Prophets and kings throughout history would have sacrificed anything to see Him and to hear His words (Luke 10:24). We can make the same observation. We have access to the Spirit of God, who has come to reside in our hearts through our faith in Jesus. The Treasure the world has always hungered for is ours—in intricate, intimate detail.

Are we casual about our knowledge of Jesus and His Word? Have we been so saturated with the message of the gospel that we take it for granted? Are we really aware that taking up God's Word to read it is to taste the riches that finite minds have sought for all history? Like farm animals with access to life's priceless pearls, we have the revelation of the all-wise God on our bookshelves and His Spirit in our hearts. Our eyes have been blessed.

Remember your Treasure. Give Him thanks today.

He turned to the disciples and said, "Blessed are the eyes that see what you have seen." LUKE 10:23

DAY 310

⚙ **A reflection on THE CROSS**
When I need to remember my utter need for God

The life of faith begins with a confession of bankruptcy. In order to accept our Savior, we must accept our need. We cannot have His righteousness without denying our own; we cannot have His holiness without confessing our sin; and we cannot receive His redemption without owning up to our bondage. We are bankrupt before Him, and fools if we do not know it.

Make no mistake—the Cross was a place of disgrace. It was the symbol of death. It was brutal and ugly, horrid and shameful. But it was God's way! From the foundation of the world, He ordained that His priceless treasure be dressed in very plain clothes.

Never despise the humble appearance of God's plan. If you're ever tempted to avoid the unattractive path God has planned, turn to Jesus on the Cross. See Him as a reminder that priceless treasures are in broken vessels.

God has united you with Christ Jesus. For our benefit God made him to be wisdom itself. Christ made us right with God; he made us pure and holy, and he freed us from sin.
I CORINTHIANS 1:30

☼ A reflection on GOD'S FAITHFULNESS
When I wonder if God is still working in my life

God seems to work with us in seasons. We may go through periods of feeling particularly close to Him, followed by periods of apparent distance. We may have times of plenty followed by times of scarcity. We can see God using our labor and blessing it, and then we see His pruning process and wonder where His blessing has gone. Or we may even willfully distance ourselves from God's work through apathy or sin. Our temptation in any of these times is to think that God is done with us. But we must resist that temptation. If we're alive, He isn't finished with us.

Our job is to be alert, to cultivate the gifts He has given us, and to persevere in the good works He has prepared for us in advance (Ephesians 2:10). There is no "falling away" too substantial for Him to restore. There is no weakness greater than His strength. Wherever we are in our walk, there is revival to be sought and work to be done. He continues to work.

I am certain that God, who began the good work within you, will continue his work until it is finally finished on the day when Christ Jesus returns. PHILIPPIANS 1:6

☼ A reflection on GUARDING MY HEART
When I don't want to be captive to my emotions

Most of us give our hearts free rein. We're under the illusion that we can't help how we feel. And as our feelings rise and fall as often as the wind changes direction, so does our life. We make decisions based on feelings and then rationalize them. We let our emotions define us. It is a dangerous way to live. We are to guard our hearts. We are to be careful about what we let into them. Our hearts cannot be an open door to unbiblical and ungodly influences. We are not to be captive to them; they are to be captive to the Word of God. We are given the responsibility of being vigilant about their content.

You may be waiting for Him to shape your heart, while He is waiting for you to guard it. He will do His part, but only you can do yours. The wisdom of Proverbs makes your vigilance the highest priority: "above all else." That is the attention we are to give to our emotional swells. It is paramount. Be on guard.

Guard your heart above all else, for it determines the course of your life. PROVERBS 4:23

☀ A reflection on GOD'S CHARACTER
When I need to reject Satan's lies about God

Satan is out to distort God's image. He lies to us about the character of God. He poisons our understanding by inspiring false philosophies, by offering false promises, and even by manipulating the Word of God to say what it doesn't really say.

We let him get away with it, don't we? Any time we question God's goodness, distort His Word, pursue unbiblical insights, or craft our own image of God to suit our own purposes, we have fallen for the lies.

The father of lies has many children. Where in this world can we turn for safety? To what solid rock may we anchor to avoid tossing around on the waves of phony concepts? Jesus gives us the answer: "You will know the truth, and the truth will set you free" (John 8:32). This truth is a Person (John 14:6). Cling to Him and believe no one else.

[Jesus said,] "I am the way, the truth, and the life. No one can come to the Father except through me." JOHN 14:6

☀ A reflection on CRYING OUT TO GOD
When I am in distress

Wake up to the fact that the almighty, overwhelming God is listening to you call. Even when you complain, He cares. More than that, He hears with a plan to act. He is not passively listening; He is preparing to answer. Wouldn't you love for Him to step into your situation? According to the Bible, He will. Watch and wait. Your distress is His concern.

Morning, noon, and night I cry out in my distress, and the LORD hears my voice. PSALM 55:17

DAY 315

☀ A reflection on GOD'S CHARACTER
When I realize I can't fully understand God

We can count on God's character. We know He is holy, righteous, omniscient, omnipotent, loving, merciful, and more. He and His Word are forever reliable. Yet no one can explain Him fully. That can be unsettling, because we like explanations. But a god we can explain isn't God. Remember that when your life seems out of control. It isn't. It is under the hand of the mysterious, mighty God.

Just as you cannot understand the path of the wind or the mystery of a tiny baby growing in its mother's womb, so you cannot understand the activity of God, who does all things. ECCLESIASTES 11:5

⚙ A reflection on GOD'S GIFTS
When I need to receive what God offers

Imagine a hungry homeless man on the sidewalk in front of an open-air restaurant. A sign reads: "Free buffet. All you can eat. Everyone welcome." Everything the man needs for the moment is offered, but he won't sit down. Perhaps he doesn't understand the sign, doesn't believe it applies to him, or feels like he's too dirty to fit in. Regardless of the reason, he hungers while others eat. Unfortunately, that's how many Christians approach God's promises. The banquet of God waits for us, but we can't relate to it, so we won't go sit down. We forget that God's promises are lavished upon us with His own Son as the guarantee.

Blessed are those who accept God's promises like children, who are too innocent to ask questions or to be suspicious of His extravagance. We have a God of enormous abundance, and we are a people of enormous need. He invites us to display our poverties before Him so He can show the world His mercies. What prevents us from receiving His bounty with open arms?

What joy for those you choose to bring near, those who live in your holy courts. What festivities await us inside your holy Temple. PSALM 65:4

☼ A reflection on BELIEF
When I want to see God's glory

It's human nature that says, "I'll believe it when I see it." Jesus says, "You'll see it when you believe it." It's one of the hardest principles for Christians to grasp. The work of almighty, sovereign God is often actually dependent on the level of our faith. It isn't that we limit Him; it's that He has limited Himself. His modus operandi in this world is to act in response to faith: the prayers of faith, the obedience of faith, the attitude of faith.

Do you find yourself in a difficult situation? Believe God, and you will see His glory. That doesn't mean that we lay out a plan of action for Him. Faith does not dictate God's method of intervention. But it certainly invites His act of intervention—in His way and in His time. When a crisis comes, do we complain that God was not watching over us, or do we watch for His glory? Our inward response might have more impact than we think.

Jesus responded, "Didn't I tell you that you would see God's glory if you believe?" JOHN 11:40

☼ A reflection on WORSHIP
When I want to offer myself to God

Wisdom begins with basing one's life on reality. "Fear of the LORD is the foundation of wisdom" (Proverbs 9:10). Why? Because fear of the Lord is based on a true understanding of who we really are and who God really is. But there is a next step. Wisdom doesn't begin and end with fear; it continues into worship. When we really understand who God is, the natural response is to offer Him whatever we can get our hands on—and all we have is ourselves.

Worship is a lifestyle, a sacrificial way of living that acknowledges every moment of every day that there is One far more worthy of our allegiance than ourselves. When His interests consistently supersede ours, and we act accordingly, we are worshiping. Live out your day mindful of whose you are. In light of who He is, this is true worship. And true worship is the wisest thing we can do.

Give your bodies to God because of all he has done for you. Let them be a living and holy sacrifice—the kind he will find acceptable. This is truly the way to worship him.
ROMANS 12:1

☼ A reflection on COMFORT
When I need to feel the Presence of the Holy Spirit

Jesus speaks often in John 14–16 about the Holy Spirit's comforting purpose. Where many translations use "Counselor," others use "Comforter." Both are appropriate. The Spirit is a comforting Counselor who promises us peace, and He is a counseling Comforter who promises to relieve our fears.

When we are unsettled, we ask a lot of "why" questions. "Why did this happen to me?" "Why does God seem so absent?" "Why doesn't God *do* something?" During these times, we must remember the promise of the Holy Spirit, a promise from a sovereign God who is "always ready to help in times of trouble" (Psalm 46:1). Faith will make His Presence—with all of His peace and comfort—real to us.

But what if this same Spirit lives within us? Not only will we have comfort and peace, we will minister to others in their trials. We will be comforting counselors and counseling comforters. We will represent "the God of all comfort" (2 Corinthians 1:3, NIV) as He ministers through us.

The Father of compassion and the God of all comfort . . . comforts us in all our troubles, so we can comfort those in any trouble with the comfort we ourselves receive from God.
2 CORINTHIANS 1:3-4, NIV

☼ A reflection on CONSISTENCY
When I'm seeking steady progress in my Christian walk

Nearly everyone has a spiritual mountaintop experience on occasion. For most of us, this is how we measure our spiritual maturity. We assume that the heights we've reached indicate the level to which we've grown. But God has a different measure of our maturity. It's not about the peaks we've scaled but our consistency between them. Learning the mind of God is not a roller-coaster experience; it's a steady climb. A peak experience will indeed give us a satisfying feeling for a while, and we'll gladly dwell on it as long as we can. But while we dwell there, we can lose sight of today's needs.

Our God is not One to be appeased periodically and ignored in the interims. His love for us is constant and persistent. His character never changes. His mercy is new every morning, and His compassion does not fail. If our minds are being renewed to be like His, isn't consistency a logical result? The blessings of discipleship and worship are found only in their constancy. Measure yourself not by your highs or lows, but by who you are in between them.

Oh, that my actions would consistently reflect your decrees!
PSALM 119:5

DAY 321

✸ A reflection on KIND WORDS
When I need encouragement

Proverbs 12:25 gives an unusual solution to anxiety: kind words. Let your life be full of them. Tell them to yourself. God's truth is kind to you, after all; rehearse it often. Use kind words with others. God's primary vehicle for expressing Himself in this world is through people. Verbally demonstrate His kindness to others. And when others offer kind words to you, accept them. God has sent them to you. Accept them, and do not be anxious.

Anxiety weighs down the heart, but a kind word cheers it up.
PROVERBS 12:25, NIV

DAY 322

✸ A reflection on LIVING BY THE SPIRIT
When I want to cultivate the Spirit in my life

Sin and self may have natural appeal, but ultimately a self-directed life is deceitful. It promises us success but delivers nothing that lasts. When we cultivate our human nature, we get more human nature; when we cultivate the Spirit, we get more of the Spirit. So sow eternal seeds. Live by the power of the Spirit. Be forever joined to the plan, the purposes, and the Person of the incorruptible God. And then enjoy reaping what you've sown.

You will always harvest what you plant. . . . Those who live to please the Spirit will harvest everlasting life from the Spirit.
GALATIANS 6:7-8

☼ A reflection on GIVING
When I want to honor God by my generosity

The purpose of all creation is to honor God. So it only makes sense that when He is honored—in the case of Proverbs 3:9-10, by our wealth and the best part of everything we have—He will grant increase and give His blessing. Honor begets more honor. Of course, this is no guarantee that those who tithe will become rich. It *is* a promise, however, that God will never be stingy with those who are generous toward Him. He always gives more than He receives. Have you stated unequivocally that you are in line with God's purpose for creation—to give Him honor?

One way to honor Him is by dedicating all of our resources to His use, giving a generous portion to His work in this world. By this He is glorified. And by this we are proven trustworthy to handle more resources. God calls us to be like Him. He has proven over and over again that He is by nature an extravagant giver. Are you?

Honor the LORD with your wealth and with the best part of everything you produce. Then he will fill your barns with grain, and your vats will overflow with good wine.
PROVERBS 3:9-10

☼ A reflection on AUTHORITY
When I need to remember that Jesus is sovereign

Wartime stories of soldiers defecting to the victorious side are common. Why? No one likes to end up on the losing side. But as Christians, we don't have that problem. We know who will win. We know who holds all authority in His hands. We know who is seated at the right hand of God and will judge the nations of the earth.

But here is the dilemma the Christian faces: the world systems seem to be winning in the short term while the ultimate Authority often seems obscured in heaven, waiting for the final minutes of the game to reveal His victory. We are tempted in the meantime to play for the short term. But we cannot. We must choose sides now.

The Christian life is playing the game with a focus on its end. We cannot support both sides. Our involvement in the mission of Christ is based on its glorious result more than its humble present. Our actions today will acknowledge whom we regard as our ultimate Authority.

Jesus came and told his disciples, "I have been given all authority in heaven and on earth." MATTHEW 28:18

☼ A reflection on OUR HEAVENLY FATHER
When I consider what it means to be a child of God

Though we grow beyond childhood in human terms, we are always God's children. We grow up spiritually, but we never grow to be independent of our heavenly Father. The carefree attitude that many children have can be ours. Why? The details are being taken care of by Someone older and wiser. He has not asked us to stay up late to worry about how to make ends meet. He has not burdened us with resolving family crises. He has let us see some of the family stress, of course, and He even asks us to play a role in handling it. But bearing the burden? Never. That's the Father's task, not ours.

We are not to ignore the burdens of life; we are to cast them into His arms. It honors God when we refuse to worry about something He has promised to do. He has never betrayed our trust. We know whose hands guard our family, and we know how secure His house is. The more we act like unburdened children, the more we prove our faith. And that always pleases our Father.

Anyone who becomes as humble as this little child is the greatest in the Kingdom of Heaven. MATTHEW 18:4

☼ A reflection on KNOWING GOD
When I consider the source of true satisfaction

Thanksgiving is usually celebrated with lavish spreads of delicious food. We know it as a day of abundance where we enjoy the bounty God has given in full measure. We should always be so grateful. But we should also realize the greater blessing. Knowing God is an infinitely worthwhile treasure. The food that Jesus provides lasts forever. Though scorned by many, it is of infinite worth. It is unimpressive to the material mind, but in the end it will be seen by all for what it is—priceless beauty and awesome privilege. Everyone—believer and unbeliever—will gaze at the gift of salvation and say, "That's what my heart really desired all along."

The best Thanksgiving satisfies for a day, at most, but it doesn't endure. It's the gratitude that lasts, not the material gifts. And it's the eternal gift that prompts eternal gratitude. If we really saw the value of each—perishable things and eternal life that endures—we'd never get the two confused.

Don't be so concerned about perishable things like food. Spend your energy seeking the eternal life that the Son of Man can give you. JOHN 6:27

☼ A reflection on THANKFULNESS
When I need to praise God in all circumstances

We often go through waves of feeling that God is distant. Sometimes the waves are prolonged—circumstances batter us, discouragement plagues us, and God seems far, far away. God's prescription for entering His Presence is to give thanks. The apostle Paul even told believers to give thanks in every circumstance (1 Thessalonians 5:18). He didn't tell them to give thanks only when the clear evidence of God's blessing is visible. He told them to give thanks always—in every situation. How can we do this? On the basis of who God is. If we know that He is good, that He is sovereign, and that He is wise, we can give thanks that He is working out His plan even in the difficult circumstances of life.

Establish in your mind a discipline of thanks. Enumerate every aspect of your life, and thank God for it. In every circumstance, choose to see it from an angle that will cultivate gratitude. God will be honored. And His Presence will be real.

Enter his gates with thanksgiving; go into his courts
with praise. Give thanks to him and praise his name.
PSALM 100:4

DAY 328

☼ A reflection on GOODNESS
When I want to be a reflection of God to the world

Most of us are busy trying to impress others with a remarkable personality, amazing skills, or our outstanding achievements. God's Spirit in us, however, will not make us flashy. He will make us good. We forget that behind every miracle, behind every teaching, behind every revelation and prophecy, there is the goodwill of God. Goodness underlies everything He does. Do you bear His goodness? Demonstrate it to someone today. Show your world what God is like.

Surely your goodness and unfailing love will pursue me all the days of my life. PSALM 23:6

DAY 329

☼ A reflection on ENEMIES
When I consider people I don't get along with

How do you treat your enemies? Do you hold grudges? Do you secretly hope that God will humble them and vindicate you? Perhaps He will. If you really believe in His goodness, you are free to let Him handle justice on your behalf. You are free to behave in unexpected and godly ways by blessing those who curse you, giving to those who have cheated you, or complimenting those who have insulted you. Treating an enemy well honors His merciful will.

If your enemies are hungry, give them food to eat.
PROVERBS 25:21

☼ A reflection on SATISFACTION
When I want to be content in God

Human nature is never satisfied. We are always waiting for the next good thing. Whatever gifts God has given us, we want more. The good thing about our constant quest for more is that, when rightly directed, we can have it. If our dissatisfaction moves us toward God and His Kingdom rather than toward temporal fulfillments, it will eventually be rewarded. God never denies those who want more of Him.

Are you dissatisfied with life? Ask yourself why. If you are filling your life with things that don't last, you will never be satisfied at all. How can you be? The things you seek are not inherently satisfying. But God is. If you are filling your life with Him (and letting Him fill your life with Himself), He will satisfy, and when you grow discontent again, He will give more. Your holy craving will drive you deeper into His Presence. That's not a problem. He is inexhaustible in His riches. We can forever explore Him, and if we want more, there will be more to find.

You satisfy me more than the richest feast. I will praise you with songs of joy. PSALM 63:5

☼ A reflection on JESUS' SECOND COMING
When I need to live in light of Jesus' return

We are often told that we are products of our past. Our biological makeup and much of our personalities result from the genetic material of our ancestors. Our decisions, our flaws, and our preferences are the result of our childhood and our social environments.

No, says Jesus. Our behavior today is to be based on our future. Our new nature has come from Him, we are being conformed to His likeness, and our deeds today are to be determined by the fact that He is coming again. We are products of a coming Kingdom, not a conditioning past.

Jesus tells His disciples to be ready at all times, like servants prepared for a returning master. Even in the dark hours, when we see unclearly and grow discouraged, we are to keep our lamps burning. We should not grow despondent if He delays. We are to serve in His household while He is away, keeping our eyes open to see Him when He returns.

Be dressed for service and keep your lamps burning, as though you were waiting for your master to return from the wedding feast. Then you will be ready to open the door and let him in the moment he arrives and knocks. LUKE 12:35-36

☸ A reflection on ABUNDANT LIFE
When I feel discouraged

It's easy in the midst of this battle we call "life" to feel downtrodden, overwhelmed, burdened, and even trapped. Yet it is not God's will for us to be bound by circumstances. It is not His will that we live discouraged lives or just function day-to-day. It is His will for us to have abundant life—a consistent, joyful celebration of the triumph we now have and will fully realize in our eternal position in Christ.

How do we get there? A big hint is given in Luke 10:20. While the enemy would have us focus on his scorpions and snakes, overwhelmed with his power, Jesus would have us looking elsewhere: on the eternal prize. Rejoicing that our names are written in heaven is the key to the burdens of life getting smaller and God getting bigger in our eyes. Our pictures are in the King's family album. *That's* abundant life.

Look, I have given you authority over all the power of the enemy, and you can walk among snakes and scorpions and crush them. Nothing will injure you. But don't rejoice because evil spirits obey you; rejoice because your names are registered in heaven. LUKE 10:19-20

⚙ **A reflection on DEPENDENCE**
When I need to be reminded of my daily need for God

True bread, heavenly bread, is given on a day-by-day basis. We cannot worship enough on Sunday to last us the whole week. The directions we got yesterday won't apply today. The daily bread principle is unalterable. We can't store up the things we need from God. We have to keep coming back for them, keep trusting Him for them, day after day after day.

Why is this so? Because God insists that we have a relationship with Him, and relationships must be maintained. He knows well that if He gives us our supplies for a week or a month, we will only seek Him once a week or once a month. The temptation is great to gather in all that we can today—physically, psychologically, emotionally, and spiritually. But the daily bread principle is always at work, in all areas. There is no loving trust when there's a full storeroom.

Just as our loved ones are not content with one "I love you" for the year, God is not content with a periodic appearance before Him. Ask for daily bread in every area of life. And come back again tomorrow.

Give us each day our daily bread. LUKE 11:3, NIV

☼ A reflection on COMMUNITY
When I want to share in the work of helping others

Rarely in Scripture is God's work between Him and only one person. He works through community. His Word defines us as His body—many parts working together as one whole—and He works through the church to reach a needy world.

What does the church do with our needy ones? Sometimes we criticize them for being needy. Sometimes we tell them to go to Jesus themselves. Sometimes we even tell them to get help first, and then they'll be suitable for meeting Jesus. We miss the whole point.

God's purpose in this world is to display His glory. Sometimes that is for one or two people to see, but usually not. Usually, He wants as many people as possible to observe His answers to prayer. Usually, He wants as many as possible to hear His stories of deliverance. Usually, He wants people who come to Him to be brought by others who believe in Him. This is our work—carrying our wounded to Jesus in faith, so that we all give praise to God.

Some people brought to him a paralyzed man on a mat. Seeing their faith, Jesus said to the paralyzed man, "Be encouraged, my child! Your sins are forgiven."

MATTHEW 9:2

DAY 335

⚙ **A reflection on ETERNAL INVESTMENTS**
When I need to devote my life to what will last

Learn to see your actions today as eternal investments.
They may not bear immediately visible profits or losses,
but the profits and losses are given an eternity to work
themselves out. Their scale can be massive. A wise word,
a timely gift, or a simple act of service can compound
daily for all eternity. God already knows their future value.
When we've been there ten thousand years, how much will
today's investments be worth? More than we can imagine.

Think about the things of heaven, not the things of earth.
COLOSSIANS 3:2

DAY 336

⚙ **A reflection on THE CROSS**
When I think of Jesus' sacrifice

What Jesus did in surrendering to the Cross was absolute foolishness in the eyes of the world. But we can see
beyond the Cross if we are wise, and we can walk toward
it with confidence. The Cross teaches us *never to exchange
eternal glory for temporary gain.* Jesus forsook the temporal because He knew the eternal. See what God has done,
learn the wisdom of the Cross, and embrace it.

God has made the wisdom of this world look foolish.
I CORINTHIANS 1:20

☼ A reflection on ETERNAL PERSPECTIVE
When I want to serve God wholeheartedly without fear

Those who sit in God's fellowship often, meditating on His mind and accepting His love, will begin to view time in terms of eternity rather than as the brief life we live on this broken planet. We will make decisions not with present security and future retirement in mind, but with "forever" in full view. The Spirit of the eternal God will fill us with eternal thoughts.

What stands in the way of this perspective? Fear. We are often afraid that we will not have enough to take care of our families and ourselves if we live "all out" for God. But we don't have to obsess about our security now when we are assured of an everlasting home that cannot be taken away. We are free to serve God at whatever cost because nothing can cost us our inheritance. We know where this life will lead us and that it will never end. Forsake fear. Maintain an eternal perspective and know that His promises are certain. We know what counts, and we can live with our gaze on the city with eternal foundations.

Abraham was confidently looking forward to a city with eternal foundations, a city designed and built by God.
HEBREWS 11:10

⚙ **A reflection on LOVING GOD**
When I am tempted to view God only as a way to improve myself

We often take a utilitarian approach to God. We want to be filled with His Spirit because it will lead to more fruitful ministry, more fulfilling relationships, and more power in our personal growth. But God is not primarily our self-help technique; He is the Lover of our souls. We should first and foremost want to have His mind and be filled with His Spirit not because it benefits us but because we love who He is.

Is your relationship with God about love? Or do you pursue God simply for the change He can bring you? If so, take a step back and try another approach. Come to God with a confession of your love for Him. If you can say it honestly, tell Him you want a deeper experience of His Presence because you love who He is—His purity, His mercy, His love, His holiness, His power, His wisdom. Do not move on to requests; bask in His character. Have fellowship with Him. Your service and your place in His Kingdom will grow out of this foundation of love.

Obey my commands and live! Guard my instructions as you guard your own eyes. PROVERBS 7:2

☀ **A reflection on PEACE**
When I want to be a peacemaker in the world

What makes for peace? The world thinks it is political agreements, law enforcement, education, economic prosperity, and more. But the real key to peace is spiritual. And the Prince of Peace is the One who holds the key. Real peace involves a change of heart, and the only thing that can really change a human heart is the gospel of Jesus. It's the only thing that fundamentally alters the fallen nature we're born with.

What can you do to create peace on this violent planet? You can try to encourage it, enforce it, legislate it, financially support it, or socially orchestrate it. But unless your efforts reach the human heart, you've only inhibited conflict, not created peace. To be a real peacemaker, you must introduce people to the only power on the planet that can change a heart from within—Jesus. His Spirit reconciles a person to God and transforms human relationships. Let His Spirit work through you. Be a peacemaker. And you—and your world—will be blessed.

God blesses those who work for peace, for they will be called the children of God. MATTHEW 5:9

DAY 340

☼ A reflection on THE HOLY SPIRIT
When I remember the power of God's Presence living in me

Next time you're trying to understand God's Word or pray according to His will, next time you're trying to overcome sin, next time you're trying to make sense of your circumstances or relieve your pain, stop and remember the assistance available to you. God is the greatest power in the universe, and He makes Himself known through faith and persistent asking. Don't settle for a faint awareness that He is there somewhere, though you're not sure where. Pound on the doors of heaven—read Luke 11:5-13 if that concept bothers you—until He's a reality experienced in your heart. Remember that Jesus would not have left us in body unless He'd planned to come back to us in Spirit, deeper and fuller than we could ever have known Him otherwise.

Jesus promised His disciples that the Holy Spirit is a gift for those persistent enough to ask for Him (Luke 11:13). So ask.

It is best for you that I go away, because if I don't, the Advocate won't come. If I do go away, then I will send him to you. JOHN 16:7

☼ A reflection on UNANSWERED PRAYER
When God seems silent

As much as we hate to admit it, we are never more attuned to God's voice than when we are in desperate need. We grow during these times more than any other. Given this, why would God possibly want to rush us through that process? Why would He hasten to answer our prayers and subvert the purpose of this experience? He knows we can learn from Him and be conformed to His image in no other way.

We see our need as a desperate situation. God designs it for an opportunity to know Him more intimately. When we are truly needy, we learn of Him as Provider. When we are really sick, we learn of Him either as Healer or as Comforter—whichever role He wants to reveal to us. We might think we are being punished by His silence. We are not. We are being rewarded. He is drawing us closer to Him, saying, "Come nearer, learn from Me, know Me as your Strength, your Defender, your Refuge." Keep praying. This is a far greater blessing than an immediate answer.

Everyone who asks, receives. Everyone who seeks, finds.
And to everyone who knocks, the door will be opened.
MATTHEW 7:8

☼ A reflection on THE CROSS
  When I need to remember that God pursues me

In God's active pursuit of humans, His character is displayed. We see the intensity of His love, the wisdom of His ways, and the power of His works. The Cross teaches us *never to forget the divine initiative*. We think we pursued God, forgetting that He supplies all revelation, all strength, and all means of knowing Him. We receive only what He has already given. As a result, we cannot celebrate our wisdom or the world's—only His.

God in his wisdom saw to it that the world would never know him through human wisdom. I CORINTHIANS 1:21

DAY 343

☼ A reflection on DELIVERANCE
  When I need to depend wholly on God

God is a Deliverer for those who recognize how vulnerable they are. "God helps those who help themselves" is a catchy saying, but it is not biblical. Rather, God helps those who know how helpless they are and who appeal to Him—on His terms—for deliverance. If we want God to be our stronghold in times of trouble, we must *depend* on God as our stronghold. The deliverance is His, and His alone.

The LORD helps them, rescuing them from the wicked. He saves them, and they find shelter in him. PSALM 37:40

DAY 344

☼ A reflection on HEALING
When I wonder about Jesus' power today

What does Jesus' healing power mean to us? It does not mean that we forever avoid the death and decay that has befallen all mankind. But it means that there is an ultimate answer to this problem. Sometimes we are given signs of it now—amazing, glorious signs of physical healing. Sometimes we die with the promise on our lips. Either way, the answer is sure. Jesus will heal.

Yes, we are the walking wounded. Sooner or later, all of us can relate. But there's a Healer who walks with us. He means for us to depend on Him with everything that's in us. He does not push us through this world simply to survive. He leads us that we might overcome. Hang on to that hope. Whether you see it today or not, His power does not fail. It cannot. Your faith has healed you, and it will always heal you. Live with His peace.

"Daughter," he said to her, "your faith has made you well. Go in peace." LUKE 8:48

☼ A reflection on DISCIPLINE
When I don't want God's correction

Our natural reaction to rebuke—from anyone, even God—is to get offended. We don't want anyone telling us what to do, and we don't think anyone has a right to do so. It's human nature to have a hard time accepting correction; after all, we are creatures looking for superficial peace and comfort. Yet we cannot afford that luxury as disciples. We begin as sinners, and we want to end up as redeemed children of God. To get there, we must endure a lot of correction along the way. Otherwise, we can never be remade into His image. Our problem is confusing God's rebuke with His disapproval. We must understand that His correction is never to condemn and always to edify. It's a painful edification, but it is well worth it.

One day we'll stand in eternity and pour undying gratitude at His feet for the difficult things we went through and the discipline He imposed on us. It will have made us more gloriously radiant in the everlasting Kingdom. Temporal pain for eternal blessing is a bargain. Always cooperate with His discipline, and thank Him for its promise.

Don't reject the LORD's discipline, and don't be upset when he corrects you. PROVERBS 3:11

☸ A reflection on WAITING
When I am impatient for God's answer

Often we look for God's direction in a matter—a career choice, a business decision, or maybe a relationship issue. We are willing to act. We'll do whatever He says. We just need to know what it is. We don't hear from Him, and then we grow impatient. And just when it seems that God has left us in a state of perpetual ambiguity, He acts. We were to wait and watch because, like the disciples after Jesus' ascension, we were yet unequipped.

Waiting is perhaps the most difficult aspect of a believer's relationship with God. Our culture emphasizes speed, efficiency, and instant gratification. We pray and then wonder at God's "silence" when His response isn't immediate. We forget the stories of Joseph, Moses, and many others who spent years in preparation for God's timing.

When we find ourselves impatient and directionless, we must remember that all of His work is done on His initiative and that He takes time to prepare us for it. Like the disciples, we are to wait and watch.

Do not leave Jerusalem, until the Father sends you the gift he promised. ACTS 1:4

☼ A reflection on GOD'S LOVE
*When I need to remember how much God cares
about me*

Is the love of God lost on you? Are you one of the many
who find it hard to believe God's love for you is unconditional? Do you find it hard to love Him back? The burden
of love is not on your shoulders, either in giving it or
receiving it. It's all about Him.

When you find it difficult to accept God's amazing,
unconditional love, meditate on His loving nature, not on
whether you are worthy of it. Consider how Someone who
defines Himself as "love" could think of you in any other
way—regardless of what you've done. And when you find
it difficult to love God with the type of worship and adora-
tion He expects, meditate on His worthiness, not on your
ability to love in return.

Love isn't mustered up, it's completely absorbed in its
object. Let Him occupy your thoughts, and love will flour-
ish. Where He's involved, it always does.

*The Father himself loves you dearly because you love me and
believe that I came from God.* JOHN 16:27

☼ A reflection on RESOURCES
When I need to invest what God has given me

What do you do with the things God has given you?

The gifts of God are not given for us to hoard. They are not even given for us to save wisely. They are given for us to invest. There will always be some risk of loss involved, and there will always be some loss of ownership on our part. But the alternative is for us to take what God has given—time, talents, skills, money, property, relationships, and more—and do absolutely nothing lasting with them. This grieves God and it shames us.

Do you see the difference between saving and investing? Saving preserves; investing multiplies. God is interested in multiplying. Since He owns everything already, He is not interested in our preserving what we have. He is interested in our using it for better purposes. We are to invest, to multiply, to see the Kingdom expand—even at great risk to ourselves. The Master will return for an accounting. What will you do with His resources today?

Each of you should use whatever gift you have received to serve others, as faithful stewards of God's grace in its various forms. I PETER 4:10, NIV

☀ A reflection on LOVE
When I want God's character to define me

Does your life bear the banner of love? Are you aware of God's great love for you? Do you have great love for Him and for others? No matter how spiritually mature a believer is, it is a false spirituality if he or she is not thoroughly saturated in love. "God is love, and all who live in love live in God, and God lives in them" (1 John 4:16). Let love, above all else, define you.

His banner over me is love. SONG OF SOLOMON 2:4, NIV

DAY 350

☀ A reflection on INTENTIONS
When I feel God calling me to action

Good, godly intentions are meant to be lived, not dreamed of. The impulses of a Spirit-filled person are a call to action. Is there anything you have always felt God might want you to do, but you have never gotten around to it? Is His agenda always a matter of "one day" to you? Put feet on your intentions. Live them well. Our wonder-working God is calling His people to action.

Faith by itself isn't enough. Unless it produces good deeds, it is dead and useless. JAMES 2:17

☀ A reflection on SPREADING THE GOSPEL
When I want to have a global view of evangelism

We like the idea of our own private Jesus. We celebrate the Bethlehem miracle as our own personal advent—not just Immanuel, God with us, but "God with me, personally." It is not wrong to understand Jesus this way; He is the Savior not only of the world but of us as individuals. But it is wrong to understand Jesus *only* this way. He is always reaching out. Jesus *is* the gospel. And the gospel does not sit still. Today, He continues to spread into the far reaches of the world. That is why He came.

Is a global focus part of our own outlook? It needs to be. The Jesus who dwells in our hearts does not sit still, and if we are sensitive to Him, He will not let us sit still either. We need to be responsive to Him when He says He wants to go farther and reach out to more people. He is always aware of the many, many sheep in this world who have no shepherd. Are you?

Jesus replied, "We must go on to other towns as well, and I will preach to them, too. That is why I came."
MARK 1:38

☼ A reflection on LIVING BY FAITH
When I am afraid to base my life on what I cannot see

The problem most of us encounter in this life of faith is that we must base our decisions, our futures, our families, our jobs—our everything, in fact—on realities we cannot see. Not only can we not see them clearly—though God will open our eyes to them more clearly if we ask—those around us cannot see them, either. When we live by faith, we can't see very far in front of us. And our family members and friends are watching. While we're barely understanding our next steps, they can't understand them at all. That can lead to ridicule and uncertainty. Just ask Moses, who was called to demand from a hostile ruler the release of a million profitable slaves. Or Elisha, who was surrounded by a vicious army, but more greatly encompassed by heavenly hosts. Or Mary, who bore the Son of God by quite unconventional—and socially unacceptable—means.

Are you afraid to live by faith? Welcome to the club. But the Faith Hall of Fame in Hebrews 11 was made of such a club. Be bold and forsake nearsightedness. Faith sees more than sight ever can.

We live by faith, not by sight. 2 CORINTHIANS 5:7, NIV

☼ A reflection on THE LAW
When I wonder how I can meet God's standards

The law that was written on stone tablets—i.e., the Ten Commandments, the sum of God's moral standard—was once an agenda for how sinful humans could be godly. No one ever fulfilled it, of course, except Jesus, but it was the right standard. It is no longer our agenda, but a description of what God does in us to make us godly. It was once an external objective; it is now an internal work of the Spirit of God. It is no longer something to strive for but a measure of what God has already done and will continue to do in our hearts.

Suppose you have failed one of the commandments. Confess it and meditate on it, but do not strive to fulfill it in your strength alone. Pray to have it fulfilled in you. The perfect Son of God lives in you. Why attempt the life He has already lived? Delight in His holiness and let Him write it on your heart.

They delight in the law of the LORD, meditating on it day and night. PSALM 1:2

DAY 354

☼ A reflection on TEMPTATION
When I wonder how I can conquer the sinful nature

Temptation is a struggle for all who have ever tried to live a godly life. Godliness doesn't come naturally to us, and we are constantly tempted with what does: ambitions, lusts, bad habits, self-interest, conflict, and more. All we have to do is let down our guard and relax for a minute, and the sinful nature quickly reminds us of the old things it offers us.

Jesus' model prayer shows us what to do: Ask God to lead you away from temptation. Cooperate with Him. Ask yourself why you can be so embracing of temptation and so hesitant in faith, when it really should be the other way around. The deceitfulness of the sinful nature is subtle. The only effective counterattack is a firm "no" and an appeal for divine assistance. It's okay to ask for that; Jesus tells us to.

Don't hide your temptations from the One who is glad to oppose them. Point them out and let Him steer you away.

Don't let us yield to temptation. LUKE 11:4

☀ A reflection on PERSECUTION
When I am surprised by the world's hostility to the gospel

Those who live as disciples in this world will get on the nerves of their culture. There is an inherently abrasive relationship between the Kingdom of God and the kingdoms of people. Why? Because God and humans are rivals for the same throne.

Jesus is an offense to the ego of this world. In our natural selves, we see ourselves as lords of our own lives. When those lives are dysfunctional, we seek to improve them. But Jesus did not come into the world to improve us. He came to rescue those who are lost, broken, and helpless. Therein lies the offense. The world cannot accept a Savior until it admits it needs saving.

"Don't be surprised at the fiery trials you are going through," Peter says (1 Peter 4:12). Know that our Savior is a threat to the prideful self-sufficiency of man. Expecting nothing else, we will be well equipped when such trials come.

God blesses you when people mock you and persecute you and lie about you and say all sorts of evil things against you because you are my followers. MATTHEW 5:11

✸ A reflection on GENTLENESS
When I want to reflect God's tenderness to the world

If the fruit of the Spirit (Galatians 5:22-23) is God's display of His character through the church to a searching world, then gentleness is one of the most needed elements of that display. The world does not know of this gentle God—it portrays Him as either viciously judgmental or blandly irrelevant. It has not seen enough examples of righteous, patient, redemptive gentleness. Be one of those examples. Find a hurting person and demonstrate God's gentle touch.

Let your gentleness be evident to all. The Lord is near.
PHILIPPIANS 4:5, NIV

DAY 357

✸ A reflection on HOPE
When I see despair in others

One of the most common maladies of our generation is hopelessness. Many people have a pervasive sense that this visible life is all there is, and it isn't very satisfying. We must not let the hopelessness of our age infect us. We are to fix our hope on eternity, and we must share that hope with an anxiety-ridden generation. They are convinced that our hope is groundless. One of the most meaningful, lasting things we can do is to tell them otherwise.

Let us hold tightly without wavering to the hope we affirm.
HEBREWS 10:23

☀ A reflection on PEACE
When I wonder what kind of peace Jesus brings

Isaiah prophesied about the coming "Prince of Peace" (9:6). The angels declared peace on earth in Luke 2:14 as they announced the coming Lord. But Jesus had a different declaration. He said He will be the source of division on earth. How can this be?

The kind of peace the world seeks is harmony on this planet. Jesus made it clear that His peace is of a different order; it reconciles God with His traitorous creatures and humanity with its holy God. It puts a new Spirit in a once-conflicted heart. It is a peace within and a peace from above, but it is not universal peace among our race. In fact, because of human rebellion, many hate Jesus.

Who would have thought that the infant in Bethlehem would be so scandalous? But no one could make the kingly claims He did without controversy. The pride of the human heart will bow to no Lord, especially One who reveals its sin. The Prince of Peace? Absolutely. But not the kind the world expects. Our peace is deeper and better—and it lasts forever.

Don't imagine that I came to bring peace to the earth! I came not to bring peace, but a sword. MATTHEW 10:34

☼ A reflection on JESUS' BIRTH
When I wonder why Jesus came

Why did Jesus come? Why did the Creator decide to clothe Himself in creation and enter this world through a young girl late one night in the company of livestock? The Bible is very clear: Jesus came to save us. And His incisive declaration in John 6:38 should tell us something about the will of God: it is good. Jesus defines it for us: "This is the will of God, that I should not lose even one of all those he has given me, but that I should raise them up at the last day" (John 6:39).

For everyone who has ever wondered how God sees him or her; for everyone who has ever doubted God's love when a prayer has gone unanswered or a life has become broken; for everyone who has cried out to God, "Are You there?" or "Do You care?", Jesus has this answer: He has come to do God's will, and His will is very, very good. Jesus came into this world as an act of divine love.

I have come down from heaven to do the will of God who sent me, not to do my own will. JOHN 6:38

⚙ **A reflection on GRACE**
When I feel unworthy to be used by God

It's quite an intimidating list: Moses the lawgiver. David, a man after God's own heart. Peter the rock. Paul the evangelist. Heroes of our faith. God's anointed. Role models we can never live up to—or so we think. It is profoundly encouraging that the great examples of faith and godliness in the Bible are not really the superhuman spiritual giants we've traditionally made them out to be.

Let's take another look at that list: Moses the murderer. David the adulterer. Peter the denier. Paul the persecutor. What churches or ministries today would accept them for service? God did. Not only did He use them in His service, He showcases them in His Word. They are trophies of His grace. So are we.

Who can claim to be beyond His grace? Even more, who can claim to be beyond His service? God delights in overcoming our flaws, in showing His power through our weakness. Rejoice in the encouragement of God, who gave us in His Word examples of faith who were as human as we are. And know this—that if His call was meant for such as these, it is meant for us.

I have come to call not those who think they are righteous, but those who know they are sinners. MATTHEW 9:13

☼ A reflection on ENVY
When I am weary of comparing myself to others

Our constant tendency is to compare ourselves to others, and comparison leads to envy. That affects the way we spend our money, our time, and our talents. It affects the careers we choose and the relationships we cultivate. This envy-rooted drive for success-by-comparison sucks us into a consuming rat race and tells us that we're never quite good enough. It stresses us out. How do we get beyond such a corrosive attitude? There can be no room for envy when we measure ourselves by how God sees us rather than by how others see us. If we are all abject sinners saved by extravagant mercy, who is there to envy? Only those who have taken hold of God's unfathomable grace, which is available in equal measure to all.

If you are eaten away by the stress of the rat race, first recognize the envy that underlies it. Then try this: perform one act per day that defies "success" as you once defined it. Choose not to impress someone; refuse to invest in an image; compliment someone you once judged. By all means, let your heart be at peace.

A heart at peace gives life to the body, but envy rots the bones.
PROVERBS 14:30, NIV

☼ A reflection on GUARDING MY MIND
When I need to fix my thoughts on what is right

It is unreasonable to think that hours of digesting unhealthy material will result in healthy minds and spirits. "You are what you eat" applies not only in the physical world, but also in the spiritual. Consuming all the wrong things will have all the wrong results—it's a natural law.

There's no way to take in junk without becoming junky, so God calls us to watch our diets. It pleases Him when we care for His temple, our bodies. But it pleases Him much more when we care for our minds. Our thought life is where His Spirit most prefers to work, shaping uncluttered hearts and imparting wisdom to uncluttered minds.

Even so, we do not tend to make a smooth highway for Him into our souls. Through our entertainment, we often let ourselves be bombarded by an incessant PR campaign for the ways of the world. Find a balance. Watch what goes into your mind. Without hindrance, let His thoughts nourish you.

Fix your thoughts on what is true, and honorable, and right, and pure, and lovely, and admirable. Think about things that are excellent and worthy of praise. PHILIPPIANS 4:8

DAY 363

☼ **A reflection on MEANING**
When I want to live for what will last

Solomon tells us in Ecclesiastes 2:1-11 what a life of investing in the temporal accomplishes: nothing. It's all meaningless, he concludes. One day we will die, and unless we've invested in the eternal, nothing remains. Contrast the futility of Ecclesiastes with the riches of the gospel of Jesus. There is an inheritance that comes from God. Multitudes miss it, but the eyes of faith can see the riches of the Kingdom of God. Learn to live for them, at all costs.

I said to myself, "Come, let's try pleasure. Let's look for the 'good things' in life." But I found that this, too, was meaningless. ECCLESIASTES 2:1

DAY 364

☼ **A reflection on TRUST**
When I want to depend on God with no safety net

God calls us to "reckless" trust, the kind that prepares no safety net and reserves nothing for a spiritually rainy day. That kind of trust, if broken, leaves no room to save face. But it can't be broken. Try to find someone God has forsaken. It's impossible! Observe His faithfulness and ask yourself: "Why *wouldn't* I trust Him wholeheartedly?" Think about it. Why not?

Those who know your name trust in you, for you, O LORD, do not abandon those who search for you. PSALM 9:10

DAY 365

☀ A reflection on BECOMING LIKE JESUS
When I want to know who Jesus really is

According to His own words and deeds as recorded in the Bible, what is Jesus like? He prefers forgiveness over condemnation; He is merciful to those in all sorts of pain; He hates hypocrisy and loves humility; He welcomes those who are honest about who they are and honest about who He is; He does amazing works and encourages His followers to do the same; and He loves the Word of God. If we call Him Teacher, we are committing to a lot: We must be like Him.

You may have a clear assumption of what a good Christian is. Scrap it. Jesus puts Himself before us and says, "*This* is what you will be like if you allow Me to fully train you. You will be different and you will be good; you will be both loved and hated; and you will be both blessed and crucified." Do not expect the Teacher to train you toward your own objectives: a comfortable life, exemption from pain, a just-above-average morality. Expect Him to train you for battle and for glory. It's His divine challenge. Are you up for it?

The student who is fully trained will become like the teacher.
LUKE 6:40

TOPICAL INDEX

Abundant Life | Days 120, 332

Accountability | Day 8

Ambition | Day 138

Approval | Days 258, 291

Attitude | Day 108

Authority | Day 324

Becoming like God | Day 98

Becoming like Jesus | Days 148-150, 172, 365

Being Drawn to God | Day 147

Belief | Days 33, 317

Blessing | Days 54, 270, 304

Blessing Others | Days 23, 146

Body of Believers | Day 254

Boldness | Day 83

Caring for the Lost | Day 142

Change | Day 186

Character | Day 86

Comfort | Day 319

Commitment | Days 107, 302

Community | Day 334

Compassion | Days 135, 233

Condemnation | Day 79

Confession | Day 121

Consistency | Day 320

Contentment | Days 244, 296

Control | Day 294

Conviction | Day 41

Crisis | Day 267

Cross | Days 89, 91, 277, 310, 336, 342

Crying Out to God | Day 314

Culture | Days 56, 118

Death | Day 43

Delighting in God | Day 31

Deliverance | Day 343

Dependence | Days 36, 222, 333

Despair | Day 188

Direction | Days 265, 297

Discernment | Day 137

Discipleship | Days 22, 84, 160, 206

Discipline | Days 166, 345

Doing Good | Day 247

Doing What Is Right | Day 164

Dreams | Day 306

Emotions | Day 117

Emptiness | Day 55

End Times | Day 67

Enemies | Days 17, 329

Envy | Day 361

Eternal Investments | Day 335

Eternal Perspective | Days 169, 178, 253, 337

Eternity | Day 280

Evangelism | Days 39, 211, 351

Evil | Day 232

Eyes | Day 136

Failure | Days 35, 175

Faith | Days 44-45, 76, 303

Faithfulness | Days 60, 154

Fear | Days 111, 183, 192

Fearing God | Day 46

Fellowship with Christ | Day 112

Finding True Life | Day 184

Flexibility | Day 199

Following Jesus | Days 58, 241

Forgiveness | Days 24, 249

Foundation | Day 126

Freedom | Days 61, 203, 226

Fruitfulness | Day 110

Future | Day 69

Gentleness | Day 356

Giving | Days 129, 177, 323

Glorifying God | Days 66, 250, 287

God's Agenda | Day 141

God's Authority | Day 134

God's Character | Days 176, 201, 313, 315

God's Direction | Day 273

God's Faithfulness | Day 311

God's Generosity | Day 153

God's Gifts | Day 316

God's Heart | Day 49, 209
God's Image | Day 262
God's Love | Days 301, 347
God's Nature | Day 78
God's Omnipresence | Day 269
God's Patience | Day 200
God's Plan | Day 4
God's Presence | Day 97
God's Protection | Day 185
God's Purposes | Day 181
God's Reality | Day 195
God's Ways | Day 68
God's Will | Days 13, 114, 223
God's Word | Days 18, 212, 245
Goodness | Day 328
Good Shepherd | Days 93, 213
Grace | Days 101, 106, 162, 196, 216, 360
Gratitude | Day 5
Greatness | Days 7, 240
Guarding My Heart | Days 26, 312
Guarding My Mind | Day 362
Healing | Day 344
Heart | Day 51
Heaven | Day 47
Heavenly Father | Days 32, 325
Holy Spirit | Days 42, 85, 255, 340
Hope | Days 292, 357
Humility | Days 14, 227
Identity | Day 115
Idolatry | Day 6
Impossible Circumstances | Day 156
Insufficiency | Day 218
Integrity | Days 171, 295
Intentions | Day 350
Intercessory Prayer | Day 197
Investing in the Kingdom | Day 144
Jesus | Days 29, 246
Jesus' Birth | Days 274, 359
Jesus' Call | Day 278
Jesus' Presence | Day 92
Jesus' Second Coming | Days 210, 305, 331

Joy | Days 72, 179, 220
Judging | Day 119
Justice | Day 128
Kind Words | Day 321
Knowing God | Days 1, 257, 309, 326
Law | Day 353
Legalism | Day 152
Life of the Spirit | Day 124
Light | Day 3
Light of the World | Day 224
Listening to God | Days 157, 187
Living by Faith | Day 352
Living by the Spirit | Day 322
Living Faith | Day 76
Living in the Spirit | Day 10
Lordship | Days 28, 167, 204, 259, 284
Lost | Day 52
Love | Days 34, 53, 349
Loving God | Days 103, 165, 198, 231, 276, 338
Loving Others | Days 9, 109, 130, 173, 239
Materialism | Day 286
Meaning | Day 363
Mercy | Days 15, 193, 234, 260, 308
Miracles | Day 264
Mission | Day 214
Money | Day 38
Motives | Days 143, 230
Needs | Days 50, 299
New Life | Day 100
Obedience | Days 159, 242, 298, 307
Offering | Day 208
Outward Focus | Day 37
Patience | Day 64
Peace | Days 30, 102 , 125, 266, 279, 339, 358
Persecution | Days 174, 355
Perseverance | Day 300
Persistence | Day 161

Poor | Day 271
Possessions | Day 248
Power of God | Days 123, 238
Prayer | Day 70
Pride | Days 217, 275, 293
Priorities | Days 16, 20, 74, 219, 236
Purpose | Day 73
Pursuing the Lost | Day 202
Refuge | Day 163
Regret | Day 2
Relying on Christ | Day 256
Renewal | Day 272
Repentance | Day 268
Reputation | Days 80, 251
Resources | Days 104, 348
Rest | Days 81-82, 182
Resurrection | Days 99, 194, 228
Rewards | Day 131
Sacrifice | Day 105
Satisfaction | Days 168, 330
Security | Days 94, 189
Seeking God | Day 205
Servanthood | Day 87
Service | Day 96
Sin | Day 132
Single-Mindedness | Day 191
Spiritual Hunger | Day 229
Spiritual Warfare | Day 122

Steadfastness | Day 75
Strength | Day 207
Struggle | Day 59
Submission | Day 252
Success | Day 282
Suffering | Days 243, 289
Taking Up My Cross | Day 90
Temptation | Day 354
Thankfulness | Day 327
Time | Days 48, 62, 225
Tragedy | Day 40
Transformation | Days 57, 288
Trials | Days 263, 281
Trust | Days 158, 190, 235, 364
Truth | Days 63, 237, 290
Unanswered Prayer | Days 27, 88, 341
Unbelief | Day 170
Unity | Days 19, 71
Victory | Day 180
Waiting | Days 140, 151, 346
Wisdom | Days 12, 215, 261
Witnessing | Day 21
Words | Days 25, 65, 221, 283
Work | Day 116
Works | Day 11
Worry | Days 95, 113, 133, 145
Worship | Days 77, 127, 139, 155, 285, 318